This year, the Young Writers' Future Voices competition proudly presents a showcase of the best poetic talent from over 42,000 up-and-coming writers nationwide.

Successful in continuing our aim of promoting writing and creativity in children, our regional anthologies give a vivid insight into the thoughts, emotions and experiences of today's younger generation, displaying their inventive writing in its originality.

The thought, effort, imagination and hard work put into each poem impressed us all and again the task of editing proved challenging due to the quality of entries received, but was nevertheless enjoyable. We hope you are as pleased as we are with the final selection and that you continue to enjoy *Future Voices From West Midlands Vol I* for many years to come.

FOREWORD

Edited by Carl Golder

FROM WEST MIDLANDS
VOL I

First published in Great Britain in 2000 by
YOUNG WRITERS
Remus House,
Coltsfoot Drive,
Woodston,
Peterborough, PE2 9JX
Telephone (01733) 890066

HB ISBN 0 75431 888 5
SB ISBN 0 75431 889 3

CONTENTS

Sarah Bailey 24
Carly Poole 25
Daniel Townsend 26
Madeleine Willson 26
James Chancellor 27
Hannah Ashley 27

Bishop Walsh School

Liam Townsend 28
Edward Sheldon 29
Vicki Taylor 30
Sam Carr 31
Christopher Bailey 32
Emma Yates 33
Maurice Foley 33
Katie O'Neill 34
Anne Young 35
James Troup 36
Sarah Cronin 36
Sophie O'Neill 37
Faye-Marie Crooke 38
Lewis Atkinson 39
Lucy Dickenson 40
Shannene Anderson 41
Benjamin Campbell 42
Peter Blowman 43
Edward Watson 43
Rachel Daniels 44
Nick Jealous 44
Catherine Taylor 45
Liam Mooney 46
Anastacia O'Donnell 47
Macius Grudzinski 48
Nicola McMullan 49
Chris Budd 50
Daniel Lambe 51
Danielle McGuire 52
Tom Hyde 53

Sean Ennis	145
Rebecca Wood	146
Leanne Rathore	147
Andrew Thornton	148
Jonathan Tomlinson	148
Nathan Jones	149
Robert Sansom	150
Paul Harwood	150
Stephen Hawkins	151
Amy Moran	152
James Donald	152
Charlotte Marks	153
Sarah Day	153
Hannah Yates	154
Stevie Beddoe	155
Charlotte Rolinson	156

Swanshurst School

Sara Khan	156
Sobiah Sheereen	157
Sophie Williams	157
Emily Finnimore	158
Jessica Harrison	158
Jane Miles	159
Rebecca Underdown	160
Helen Ginnis	160
Jenny Boilestad	161
Emma Willis	161
Jainey Mun	162
Megan Owen	163

Windsor High School

Kyle Newton	163
Lisa Bloomer	164
Claire Weale	164
Thomas Henderson	165
David James Sutton	166
Matthew Peniket	166

The Poems

FOOTBALL

My brother is a football fan
He supports the local team
For them to win the league
It is his best dream.

They are bottom of the league
They think they still have a chance
But until they start scoring goals
They may as well be in a trance.

They have some new players
I hope they are some good
By putting the ball in
The back of the net
Just like they should.

Nikki Gough (13)
Alumwell Comprehensive School

THE SNOW

The snow is falling,
The wind is blowing,
It's very cold outside.

We all rush out to build a snowman,
That's what it's all about,
Freezing hands and feet,
Numb all the time.

Time to go in for dinner
As the snow starts to melt,
Must get back outside
Before it all runs out!

Anna Starkey (13)
Alumwell Comprehensive School

THE FUTURE

The future world
A future whirl
We dodge all that the future hurls.

A future hope,
A future dream,
A place where robots reign supreme.

The future seems so far away,
Will ET visit every day?
He'll stay to chat
And have some tea
With you and him and her and me.

The future's far away it seems
So for now I'll go there
In my dreams.

Stuart Davies (13)
Alumwell Comprehensive School

FUTURE VOICES

'Miaow' comes from here,
'Woof' comes from there,
What can you hear?
A row from everywhere.

'Sss' comes from here,
'Squeak' comes from there,
What do you hear?
Squeak from everywhere.

'Moo' comes from here,
'Baa' comes from there,
What do you hear?
'Moo' and 'baa' from everywhere.

'Atchoo' comes from here,
A cough comes from there,
What do you hear?
Voices everywhere.

Nadeem Abas Banaras (13)
Alumwell Comprehensive School

THE DAY AFTER SCHOOL

I was walking home from school,
Acting really cool,
Then I went to play pool,
With a mate of mine from school.

After the game of pool,
With the mate of mine from school,
We went to visit the cafe,
We thought we'd have a laugh - hey?

In there was a biker,
Chatting up a hiker,
Dressed up all in leather,
Giving the girl a feather.

Suckdeep Singh Kairo (13)
Alumwell Comprehensive School

IMAGINE

Imagine playgrounds where children no longer play,
Forgotten images of yesterday.
Imagine someone took all the teddies away,
Because the children no longer wished to play.
Caught in a computer programme,
Snatched from their cots by Microsoft monsters,
Can only be switched on and saved,
But what if someone pressed and erased?
No need for Blyton, Tigger or Pooh,
Fireman Sam, Walt Disney and Christmas too,
Only plotters, scanners and microchips,
No soft play mats because no one slips,
So keep alive life's traditions,
Be seen and be heard,
Because a childless planet except on screen
Like the thoughts above seem absurd.

Tabitha Lloyd (12)
Arthur Terry School

OPEN THE DOOR TO THE FUTURE

Close the door of the past,
Open the bright new door,
Step inside the magical future.
Leave the past behind you,
Look at what the future could bring,
Make it positive and happy,
Instead of boring.

The millennium is coming!

Samantha Dobbie (12)
Arthur Terry School

HOPE FOR CHANGE

H ungry starving children.
O n the streets with no home to go to.
P oor health and not . . .
E ven any family or friends.

F rightened to be alive but afraid to die.
O ften having to steal to survive.
R eally wanting a nice comfortable life
   instead of living in a cardboard box.

C an you tell me if someone was begging
   would you help them?
H ow would you cope?
A person can buy a man a fish and feed him
   for a day or teach a man to fish and feed
   him for life.
N o one would want to live a life alone.
G iving a little instead of always taking.
E nding a life of pain and sadness.

Philippa Joanne Ford (13)
Arthur Terry School

THE SCREAM

S uicide is just around the corner,
C an you feel the tension and stress?
R aging fear crashing through my brain,
E ndless nightmares trapped in my mind,
A nyone, can you hear me?
M eet me in heaven someone.

     Ahhh!

Jonathan Abou (12)
Arthur Terry School

AS I HIDE MYSELF

All these years
I've hidden all my fears,
I walk alone
Humming my private drone,
As I hide myself.

I stand in the corner,
I sit by the phone,
Never speaking, never talking,
No one smiles at me,
As I hide myself.

I never get served,
I'm tired, weak and hungry,
My life is disturbed
But people just don't care,
As I hide myself.

I've walked for many miles,
The terrain is always the same,
It's disturbed and hostile,
I'm a nocturnal creature now,
I have to lie low,
As I hide myself.

People call me . . .
But I must not repeat,
Every day it happens,
Someone throw me a lifeline,
As I hide myself.

Is it because of my religion?
Is it because of my colour?
They're white,
As I turn my back
You'll see I'm black,
As I reveal myself!

James Turner (12)
Arthur Terry School

THE SCREAM

Henry the VIII was a mean old chap
He always wore that feathered hat.
He got rid of all his wives,
Except for one and she just died.
He had a son from his third wife,
She popped her clogs and then she died.
His son grew up to be a sickly lad
And then ended up like his dad.

Adam Czaicki (12)
Arthur Terry School

I HAVE A DREAM

I have a dream that life would be
As calm as a turquoise sea.
That missiles, bombs, mines and guns
Would be exchanged for sweets and buns.
Homeless children would then see
Their homes and all their family.
I have a dream and it will be
A dream come true - you'll see.

Carly Taylor (12)
Arthur Terry School

THE ORANG-UTANS

Why do they look so, so sad,
Their eyes so low, their mouths so dragged?
Moved from their homes by brutal force
Because some weirdo burnt their house to the floor.
This makes me sad for the orang-utans, I suppose
Because they are always in captivity and not in their homes.
Being fed lemon through the cold grey bars,
Having oranges and apples thrown from a jar.
One day I think orang-utans will roam
With a smile on their faces and joy in their hearts.
Long, long ago orang-utans were safe,
They could roam the big forests without fear or hate,
But now it has all changed, the forests have gone.
The orang-utan must think we have got no brains,
This brings me pain to see them so sad,
Killing their forests we must be so, so mad.

Chris Morgan (13)
Arthur Terry School

EXOTIC GOODS

S   harks' jaws
L   eopard skin
A   lligator leather
U   kill them all
G   orillas' hands
H   abitat ruined
T   ortoise shells
E   lephant tusks
R   eason why? I don't know.

Matt Sellman (13)
Arthur Terry School

THE MILLENNIUM BUG

What is the Millennium Bug?
Will it be long and slimy like a big, fat slug?
Will it jump through the grass like a green grasshopper
Or croak like a frog in a big, deep voice?

Tell me if you've touched a Millennium Bug,
Is it scary or rough like an elephant's trunk?
Does it glide through the sky
Or perhaps it crawls?
Maybe it lives in trees
Or underground where it's dark and scary?

Have you got a Millennium Bug?
Does it bark like a dog?
Does it purr like a cat?
Is it hairy like a hamster?
Perhaps it squawks like a parrot perched in its cage?

How does the Millennium Bug sound?
It could sound like a small winter robin,
It might sound like a cow in a field.
It may sound like a pig in the farmyard,
Or a snake hissing as it hunts for food.

There are many animals in the world today,
They're beautiful and scary in different kinds of ways.
The Millennium Bug won't be long like a slug,
It certainly won't sound like a deep voiced frog.

Only cats should purr,
Only dogs should bark.
But the future of animals on Earth is a big question mark!

Alun Evans (13)
Arthur Terry School

ANOTHER DAY

Ring, ring my alarm clock goes,
Oh no, not school again.
I get washed and think about
How they always seem to shout.

Every day when I get to school,
Oh boy, why are they so cruel?
They make fun of me because I'm black,
All day long they seem to attack.

Why me, I say in my head,
Oh, sometimes I wish I was dead.
I'm made fun of, when I speak,
All the time they call me a freak.

I wish these bullies would leave me alone,
They even torture me on the phone.
They pinch my lunch and my money
And they even think it's funny.

They laugh at me because of my skin,
They all have committed a deadly sin.
Most of them put things in my hair,
They call me 'Afro man who killed a bear'.

I sometimes think to myself, why me?
But then I sink down miserably.
I suppose they have nothing better to do,
But put me in pain and so I hide in the loo.

Home and school I can't get away,
Every single month and every single day.
I try to act really cool,
But then they think that I'm a fool.

Killing myself is what I think about,
I'm sure this is the only way out.

Robin Reeves (13)
Arthur Terry School

HOPES FOR CHANGE - I WAS WATCHING THE TV THE OTHER DAY . . .

It really upset me to see
Children living in poverty,
These days children do drugs,
Not to mention those young thugs,
Sometimes ten will live in a house,
Along with cats, dogs and one pet mouse,
Those pesky kids skip school,
It really makes their teacher drool,
They stay out from dusk to dawn
Making those policemen mourn,
Then out of the shadows I seem to see
A hope for change called New Labour,
Everyone voted on their promises
And after three years nothing,
The future's dull,
The future's bleak
And it really upsets me to see,
Children living in poverty.

Sean Taylor (13)
Arthur Terry School

BABOON

If you could look in the mirror
And tell me what you see,
A proud and kingly creature
Towering over me.

Your hands are like two gripping claws
Designed to help you climb,
Your teeth are like sharp, pointed rock,
Worn by the tide of time.

Living in the jungle
You're always on your guard,
Patient and attentive,
Although your life is hard.

And yet you seem so knowing,
So noble and so free,
I cannot help but wonder,
If you're better off than me.

Elizabeth Stainforth (13)
Arthur Terry School

BASIL

You look at me and say I'm sweet,
My ears cocked up and tail curled neat,
I'm ginger and have creamish feet,
They always give me lots to eat.
My tail's so long I chase it round,
With stripes of cream I'm easily found.
Eyes of brown all clear and bright,
They have to be so I can see at night.

Sarah Hale (12)
Arthur Terry School

FEAR THROUGH THE EYES OF A FOREST

A cloud of smog covers the sky,
The trees sway,
Animals hide,
Through the forest comes a noise,
It comes closer and closer until in view,
A monster so big and full of fumes,
Now the forest is on its knees,
But still it eats everything that it sees,
So the forest strikes back with all its might,
And the war continues into the night,
The end is near,
The fear has gone,
But no one knows who has won.

Laura Conway (13)
Arthur Terry School

I HAD A DREAM

I had a dream,
that people wouldn't hunt the elephants for their ivory tusks
and that people wouldn't kill snakes for their skin so that
people can have shoes,
I wish that birds and fish wouldn't die because of pollution
in their homes,
I wish that people wouldn't murder people to get back at them for
something they've done wrong,
Just keep the world a better place to live in for our children's,
children's children,
I had a dream that my future would be like this.

Chantelle Canning (13)
Arthur Terry School

GM CROPS

GM food is it good? Is it bad?
The government's telling us it's safe but is it?
Is it damaging normal plants and crops,
Fields full of science's flops,
What will be next
We all wonder?
Maybe plants having babies
Or crops having rabies.
Is this the future for food?
Giant carrots
Full of juice, full of colours?
Protesters trample down the crops,
You wonder why
It's such a big lie?
The farmers complain
In all their vain
On the television
We all get bored,
GM good, GM bad,
The government's telling us it's safe
but is it?

Peter Skidmore (13)
Arthur Terry Schoo

THE ALIEN

This alien's name is Cozmo,
He has his own spacepod,
He has travelled many miles
From the planet known as Zod.

He seems quite hard to understand,
He blabbers when he talks,
He has long legs and spiky feet,
He wiggles when he walks.

You won't be scared, he seems quite nice,
With his wonderful bulging eyes,
He has no hair and is missing a nose
And he's not that big in size.

Rachael Beaman (13)
Arthur Terry School

MILLENNIUM

What does the millennium hold?
Will you want to keep it or should it be sold?
As the party begins
You can hear some people laugh and sing.

They all shout 5, 4, 3, 2, 1.
There are cheers of joy from the crowd,
But some of the neighbours don't think this is allowed,
They decided to go to bed,
But what should they do instead?

The world's faces turn to their clock,
When as the Millennium Bug kicks in,
Is it a slug, which crawls in the bin?

I crawl over to watch the news,
Only to find I have blown a fuse.
What's the fuss, what's changed?
The new millennium is just the same.

Geoff Cross (13)
Arthur Terry School

THE GREAT ESCAPE

The black dark bars were holding me in,
Oh what a stench from that disgusting bin,
When I get out I'll go to church,
But all I need now is a really big burp.
It's a very small cell,
But I wish I was down the dell,
If I hadn't fell who knows where I'd be now,
My cellmate is a real bore,
I want to leave and go out that door.
We need a plan so I'll ask Dan,
Look the guard is asleep,
Now is your chance to go and flee deep,
You grab his keys while I go for a pee.
Have you got the keys? Good I'll see if the coast is clear,
I can't wait until I have a beer,
But I shouldn't have killed that goddamn deer,
There's one policeman walking around,
Oi Dan get that gun, you're going to kill him.
Bang, bang said the gun,
We ran through the door and on and on,
Oh no, we're at the end of the line,
Wait there's a passage, come on let's go.
This is wrong, if we get out we'll soon be found,
Come on, just don't make a sound,
We crawled through the passage,
Where are we?
Neee naaawww, we came right under the spotlight,
The guards came running around,
Well, back in our cells we are,
But it was fun and we got quite far.

Lee Smith (13)
Arthur Terry School

WHAT IS LIFE?

Animating noise, anonymous accounts?
Battles being bold, blasting badness?
Cruelty to creatures, be cruel to be kind?
Devastating disaster, dying, disloyal darkness?
E is for end, everlasting illusions?
Furious fighting, frightening fury?
Giant greenery, guessing fate?
Homeless hope hunter's hide?
Ivory ornaments, money increase?
(Or just jail?)
Jungles gone, cities won?
Killing for kindness? Kings and queens?
Leering lions, live lustful lives?
Murdering mayhem, making mysteries?
Never knowing, nosy nastiness?
Opinions hurt, opinions open?
Pollution peering, people's poverty?
Quakes quickly cause calamity in countries?
Rare releases, respectful requirements?
Shimmering stars, sleeping sky?
Traitorous time, not enough?
Under strain, unfortunate pain?
Vicious vain, vague violence?
Whales wondering and whalers wanting?
Xenophobia?
Yesterday - the worker of today is different from the
worker of yesterday?
Zest for life?
So many different reasons for just one word
Life!

Katherine Abrahams (13)
Arthur Terry School

ANIMAL CRUELTY

Don't be cruel to animals,
Animals are sacred things,
Tame, sweet and gentle,
They're innocent little things,
Don't be like the circuses,
They don't even care,
The way they beat the animals,
They must be going spare.

Locked in their tiny little cages,
With no comfort at all,
They run around in circles,
Until someone opens the door.

Their face fills with excitement,
Until suddenly comes a roar,
The whip flies through the air,
It hits its back,
It looks sore.

The animal limps back into the cage,
With red lines across its skin,
Surely it's against the law,
But I know I cant do anything.

Aaron Meikle (13)
Arthur Terry School

A POEM ABOUT THE ECLIPSE

Here we are in Cornwall
Waiting to view the eclipse.
I'll never see one again
So I didn't want to give it a miss.

Everyone has special glasses on,
To protect their eyes.
And everyone's attention is focused
On the skies.

The birds have stopped singing
And everybody's standing still.
There's not a sound to be heard
On this giant hill.

You can see the sun with the
Moon in the way,
What an amazing sight,
That I could look at all day.

But it had to come to an end,
All good things do.
But at least I can say I've seen the eclipse,
Can you?

Paul Jobson (13)
Arthur Terry School

MILLENNIUM HELL

What will the future hold?
Silver metal, ice cold.
Millennium Bug: zaps away minds,
Spacesuits by Calvin Klein,
Hospital is run by clumps of metal,
Forget microwave ovens, forget the kettle.
Pick up a pen and you'll get a slap,
You will be told when to eat or nap.
Forget the cars, trucks and bus,
We're talking spaceships, there'll be no fuss.
Mean metal motors are munching,
Away with the mind, our lives are crunching.
The millennium holds nothing but change,
Flashing lights, murder and rage.
Minds focused on the Millennium Dome,
A bang at twelve what happened? Our home
Falling down a long black hole!
Another big bang, no brain, no soul,
Whirling through the vortex zone,
Back we go, but we're not alone.
To 1000AD to relive the past,
Is it drama? Are we the cast?
That's what we ask, but it's all true,
We settle down, finding a clue.
Then we drink the water and eat the wheat,
Covered in rags from head to feet,
We live our millennium until we are dead,
Never escaping, sick in the head.
Is it real? A dream with a fright?
Find out for yourself on millennium night.

Jennifer Smith (14)
Arthur Terry School

Pain

No one expected it,
How could it happen?
Why did it happen?

I am trapped,
I won't be saved,
I can hear them calling for me,
Too weak to answer.

We weren't prepared.
We weren't expecting,
It happened to others,
Never to us.

Blood in my mouth,
Eyes burning,
Can see the splintered bone
Tearing through my leg,
A rusty razor ripping through a
Chunk of meat,
What's the point in fighting?

I can't feel my legs,
Water freezing water
Numbing my body,
It doesn't fool me.

I know there's something
Piercing my skin,
I can feel parts of my spine shattered,
I know I will never walk again.

I know I will never breathe again.

Richard Kelly (13)
Arthur Terry School

ALL IS QUIET

All is quiet,
The only thing you can hear is the little pattering
Feet of the hungry squirrel,
Tiptoeing over the crumbling frostbitten leaves.

He's collecting his bundle of food,
Patting down the soil where he buried his last acorn,
His pouches are full with nuts and berries
And he's getting ready for the long winter ahead.

He'll hibernate, then every few weeks
He'll wake up to the early morning sun,
To say good morning and have a nibble
On a juicy cranberry, wishing spring will be soon.

So once more in the early morning frost
You can hear the little pattering feet of the
Hungry squirrel.

Emma Juxon (13)
Arthur Terry School

THE FUTURE

The future will be full of flying cars.
The future will have the cure for the common cold.
The future will be full of peace, no fighting, no wars at all.
The people will be healthy and all have a home.
There will be holidays to Mars, the moon and Saturn.
The ozone layer will be put to right.
The Millennium Dome will be a blast.
Pollution will be gone for good and the world will be greener.

Adam Isdale (12)
Arthur Terry School

BULLIED TO DEATH

Waiting beyond the gate
To jump at him,
I guess he's just their bait
Because he's a little dim.

He comes out with a black eye
And a bruised leg,
He doesn't look like he could fly,
He looks more like the dead.

He won't tell Mom and Dad,
But they can tell
By the way he's always sad
And not very well.

That was last March,
I now have no brother,
They went too far,
I'll never have another.

I look at his grave,
He died last year,
I should have helped you Dave,
You will always be near.

Katherine Burns (13)
Arthur Terry School

SEASONS

Seasons, they come, they go,
You get four seasons,
Autumn, winter, spring and summer,
All of them have different weather.

In the autumn, it's the beginning of winter,
The leaves start coming off,
It starts to get cold,
You then start to wrap up ready for winter.

In the winter you get cold,
You get different weather,
Like rain, wind, snow, hail and fog,
The fog you can't see and you might trip over a log!

In the spring you get sun,
New plants arrive, there are new baby animals,
New piglets are pink and sweet
And new baby lambs spring with happiness.

In the summer it is blazing hot,
You are cold, *not!*
You're on holiday on the beach, the pool anything,
You want to go to the beach to go in the sea,
Just be careful that you don't get stung by a bee!

Sarah Bailey (13)
Arthur Terry School

BULLY

The break bell sounds,
My heart pounds.
They're out there waiting and I'm the bait,
I just can't wait.
Why me? What have I done?
I knew today I shouldn't have come.
I stepped outside frozen,
Why's it me they've chosen.
They begin to circle me
Like vultures looking for tea.
They shout and push
Like they're in a rush.
They scream and shout,
But what about?
They move in closer and breathe down my neck,
It's cold, oh heck!
Fists are ready,
Take it steady.
They crowd around and . . .
The break bell sounds,
My heart pounds.

Carly Poole (14)
Arthur Terry School

DEFORESTATION

It upsets me to see trees being cut down,
One day they were green, but now they are brown,
There used to be animals, pandas and snakes,
But now it is empty, just fast draining lakes.

There used to be wildlife, beautiful birds,
But now all is quiet, as the forest slowly burns,
You could once hear the voices of the great trees that stand,
But now they are not heard, it's just bare open land.

It was once a different world,
A lovely colour of green,
But now there is nothing, nothing to be seen.

There used to be plants, nature and trees,
But now all is gone, nothing left but the leaves,
It really upsets me to see the trees being cut down,
One day they were green,
But now . . . just brown.

Daniel Townsend (13)
Arthur Terry School

TRAGEDY

Silence, starvation, sadness
Among the place where the trees once were.
Tragedy,
The trees are no more,
The hills are empty now,
Time to go home,
It's not fun anymore,
On and on this story goes, no more.

Madeleine Willson (13)
Arthur Terry School

MILLENNIUM BABY

That's my little brother, just ten minutes old,
Already looking for something
To bite and suck and hold.
That's my little brother already going bald,
I can't just call him brother,
So what should he be called?

My brother was born
On the 31st of December,
And that's the day I really remember.

James Chancellor (13)
Arthur Terry School

CHANGE

What change?
Is anything changing?
What is going to change?
Is anything going to change?
Is change good?
Is change bad?
Change makes a difference, an alteration.
Change is a replacement of something else.
Can you exchange change?
The world may be changing,
But are we changing with it?

Hannah Ashley (14)
Arthur Terry School

SHOW OFF SAM

Sam with his shades on
Walkin' down the street,
Don't give a damn
About the people he meets.
He's got attitude
That everybody hates,
Thinkin' he's a cool dude
But he ain't got no mates!
Sam with his shades on
Struttin' across the road,
Sees a bunch of women
And puts himself in mode.
Doesn't see a lamppost,
Walks straight into it,
He falls to the ground
In a pile of poo!
Sam without his shades on
With a bandage on his head,
Smells like a skunk
Wishin' he was dead.
But now he's learnt his lesson
That he's no dude,
Cause without his smelly clothes
He's just nude!

Liam Townsend (12)
Bishop Walsh School

Mobile Mad Mike

Mike with his mobile
clipped onto his belt,
ring-a-ring-a-ringing,
or that's how it felt.
His hand reached down
to press the off key.
But it wouldn't turn off,
oh, leave it be!
Mike with his mobile
walked onto the train,
and he sat down,
by a man with a cane.
Ring-a-ring-ring,
and it didn't stop there,
Mike let out a moan
but he didn't care.
Mike without his mobile,
sitting up in bed,
he felt a-ringing
inside his head.
'You'll soon digest it,'
the doctor laughed,
'A phone in your stomach,
that's a joke and a half!'

Edward Sheldon (12)
Bishop Walsh School

JACK

Jack was a little kitten
Born August '95
He purred and purred
But miaowed and miaowed
As if to say 'I'm alive!'

Jack used to go to sleep,
In every possible place.
He'd run round and round
To find somewhere
As if it were a race.

When his owners got up in the morning,
There he was, at the door.
He purred and purred
But miaowed and miaowed
As he rolled across the floor.

Jack's favourite food was Felix,
He ate one tin a day.
He purred and purred
But miaowed and miaowed
As if to say, 'Dinner time. Wahey!'

'Jack, Jack!' his owners shouted,
To call him in at night.
Not all the time,
Did he come
Which gave his owners a fright.

Jack was a big cat,
Died September '97.
He didn't purr and purr
Or miaow and miaow
He just went to heaven.

Vicki Taylor (13)
Bishop Walsh School

MUTLEY THE MENACING MUTT

Mutley the mutt,
His tail up high
Barked at a kid and made him cry,
The mum went mad, shouted at a high
But Mutley just stared at the big blue sky.
So off he went trekking down the street
Trying to find somethin' he could bark at or eat.

Mutley the mutt
Went a bit too far,
Barked at a policeman:
Now behind bars.
Poor old Mutley, nothing to eat, just a bowl of
Water and a little orange sweet.

Mutley the mutt
Was sentenced to life,
He didn't know what he'd done so he testified.
Poor old Mutley lying in his cell,
Literally living in a living hell,
Nothing to do and nowhere to dwell,
Poor old Mutley we're glad you're in hell.

Sam Carr (12)
Bishop Walsh School

MARK'S MOBILE

Mark with his mobile
Cruising down the road,
Ignoring everybody
Talking on the phone.

Mark with his mobile
Talking real loud,
Not looking where he goes
Staring at the ground.

Mark with his mobile
Trying to look good,
But everybody knows
He's just a dud.

Mark with his mobile
Doesn't know what's happening around,
Gets knocked off his feet
And lands on the ground.

Mark with his mobile
Lying in the road,
I think he forgot to use
The Highway Code.

Mark without his mobile
Now I think he knows,
Not to talk
While he's crossing the road.

Christopher Bailey (12)
Bishop Walsh School

SEAN THE SHOW-OFF

Sean the show-off
Walking down the road
Really needs a girlfriend
Acting like a toad.
He thinks he's got the power
He thinks he rules the universe
But when he starts to show off
It really turns out worse.
Sean the show-off
Met a nice girl
Her name was Jenny
His brain was in a whirl.
She started to talk
He didn't know what to do
So he kept on walking
And stood on her shoe.
Sean not such a show-off
Came out in a sweat
And before he knew it
His pants were wet.

Emma Yates (12)
Bishop Walsh School

SPIDY!

I want to get rid of that big fat hairy spider,
I want to escape on that hang-glider,
I want to call in the exterminator,
I want to act like the Terminator,
I want to act really calm
I want to . . . ahhh! It's on my palm!

Maurice Foley (13)
Bishop Walsh School

MIKEY'S MISHAP

Mikey with his mobile
Struttin' down the street,
Payin' no attention
To the people that he'd meet,
By ignorin' other passers-by
He thinks he's a really cool guy.

Mikey with his mobile
Tuned in night and day,
Any other concerns
Are always put at bay,
His ear is always by the phone,
It looks as if there ain't no one home.

Mikey with his mobile
Talkin' to his plastic,
Skidded and fell
On a piece of elastic,
'Where's my mobile?' they heard him mutter,
The mobile then shattered in the gutter.

Mikey without his mobile
Standin' all alone,
Life'll never be the same
Without his mobile phone,
Orange and Cellnet are gone forever,
ET phone home, it's now or never!

Katie O'Neill (13)
Bishop Walsh School

ROLLERBLADING ROSY

Rollerblading Rosy
Gliding through the park
Really going fast
Even when it's dark
Showing off real bad
Thinks she is so cool
People think she's mad.

Rollerblading Rosy
Going much too fast
Can't really see too well
What is going past
Whizzing round and round
Now everybody knows
(Well, most people anyway)
The tale of rolling Rose.

Rollerblading Rosy
Didn't see no tree
Couldn't stop in time
Now she's offering for free
Her whizzing rollerblades
That made Rollerblading Rosy
Go straight into a tree.

Anne Young (12)
Bishop Walsh School

Jittery Jamie's Mishap

Jamie with his ball
Kickin' down the street
Pays no attention to
People that he meets.
Jamie with his ball
Knocked it way too far
Ran across the road
Straight into a car.
He manages to crawl along
To the other side
To get help from a man
Who takes him for a ride.
Jamie's in hospital
Lying on the bed
Thinkin' 'bout the Man U match
He's glad he isn't dead.

James Troup (12)
Bishop Walsh School

Bradley And His Bicycle

Bradley and his bicycle
Riding through the town
Up the curbs and over bumps
Riding up and down.

Bradley and his bicycle
Riding down the road
Not looking where he was going
And run over a toad.

Bradley off his bicycle
Lying in the street
He saw the toad and tried to help
As he clambered to his feet.

Bradley on his bicycle
Riding very slow
By now he has learnt his lesson
And is a'watching where he goes.

Sarah Cronin (12)
Bishop Walsh School

TV

TV stands for television,
A wondrous thing it is.
It shows my favourite programmes
Shows I never miss.
I sit down and relax
And sink into the chair
I focus on the TV
Until my eyes go square.
I pick up the remote
And switch the TV on.
I slip into another world
And all other thoughts are gone.
What will it be this evening
A drama, comedy or soap?
Or will it be something better,
All I can do is hope!

Sophie O'Neill (13)
Bishop Walsh School

GRANNY VS TIMMY

Granny's a hoblin',
Hoblin' with her Zimmer,
Makin' her way to Sainsburys,
To fetch her dinner
And there's little Timmy,
Skating down the road,
All the Granny's say
'He's an ignorant little toad.'

Granny's still a hoblin',
Hoblin' down that road
And Timmy's skatin',
Skating down that road,
He's a brooming and a wizzin',
Like a rocket into space
And out stepped granny,
Crash, bang, wallop,
They're a hospital case.

Granny's a fumin',
Walkin' down the street,
When out comes Timmy,
The last person she wants to meet,
His head hung in shame,
But he's wizzin' just the same,
When Granny stuck out her zimmer,
He hit the deck, oh what a shame.

Faye-Marie Crooke (12)
Bishop Walsh School

MICHAEL'S MOBILE MISHAP

Michael with his mobile,
Nosin' down the street.
Just will ignore
The people that he meets.

Michael with his mobile
Him crossin' the street
Don't really care about
Cars stoppin' at his feet.

Talkin' in his mobile,
Turnin' up the sound.
Him not aware
Of what's goin' on around.

Michael with his mobile,
Just ignored a car.
Gets knocked over
And knocked very far.

Michael in hospital,
His mum worried sick
Him in intensive care.
She thinkin' that he's thick.

Michael got no mobile
Limpin' down the street.
A bandage on his leg
And another on his feet.

Michael got no mobile
It ended up bust.
Now he knows his eyes and ears
Are senses he can trust.

Lewis Atkinson (12)
Bishop Walsh School

MARTIN ON HIS MOBILE

Martin on his mobile,
On his way to school
Talkin' to his girlfriend
Lookin' real cool.

Martin on his mobile
Strutin' down the street
Pushin' through the crowds
Steppin' on their feet.

Martin on his mobile
Causing a big fuss
Chattin' on his phone
Didn't see no bus!

Martin on his mobile
Bill's gonna cost a bomb
Thought that he was cool
But obviously he was wrong!

Martin on his mobile
Stepped out in the road
Along came the bus
But little did he know . . .
Crash!

Martin without his mobile
Drawing quite a crowd
Lying in the road
Now is he so proud?

Lucy Dickenson (12)
Bishop Walsh School

FRANK WITH HIS FOOTBALL

Frank with his football
Kickin' down the street,
Doin' kickups and headers
And holding it with his feet.

Frank with his football
Walkin' down the street
Lookin' for his friends
He's supposed to meet.

Frank with his football
Finally sees his friends,
Wondering to himself
Will this conversation end?

Frank with his football
Plays it every day,
Likes to shoot some goals
In a very skilled way.

Frank with his football
He is very vain
Even shows his skills off
When he's in the rain.

Shannene Anderson (12)
Bishop Walsh School

RODNEY WITH HIS ROLLERBLADES

Rodney with his rollerblades,
racin' down the street,
thinkin' he's a dapper,
with his great big feet,
jumpin' over hedges,
missin' all the people,
crashin' up the kerb
and stampin' on the steeple.

Rodney with his rollerblades,
cruisin' down the road,
listenin' to his music,
a pluggin' in the mode,
checkin' out the girlies,
struttin' down the street,
crashin' to the ground,
where all the people meet.

Rodney with his rollerblades,
ridin' down the track,
listenin' for the sound,
while lyin' on his back,
no fear of the train,
a comin' faster and faster,
tootin' on the horn,
with his master's blaster.

Benjamin Campbell (12)
Bishop Walsh School

INJECTIONS

I am afraid of needles,
Especially the TB and the measles,
Whenever I see one, I go all hot,
I try and remain calm and think I've forgot,
Then the nurse says 'It will not hurt!'
But I think it will, my arm will cut open and blood will spurt,
Then I feel it when it goes in,
It's the pain of a sharp shiny pin.
I faint and fall to the floor,
Wake up with a head bruised and sore,
But then I realise it's not so bad,
I am relieved, happy and glad,
But then I remember the pain of needles,
I am afraid of needles.

Peter Blowman (13)
Bishop Walsh School

RATS, I HATE RATS!

Rats, rats how I hate those creatures,
Rats, rats, I hate all their features.
I saw one once, it just looked me in my eye
I was so nervous, I wanted to cry,
It stood there staring at me
It charged toward with stealth
Its beady eyes stared me out
I jumped up and began to shout
Aghh! Aghh! A rat, a rat,
Then when I landed, the rat was now flat,
I look at my foot who'd have a clue
That, that's a rat squashed there on my shoe.

Edward Watson (13)
Bishop Walsh School

ROBERT WITH HIS READING BOOK

Robert with his reading book
Walking down the road,
Never stops reading
'Cause he's in the mode.
Robert with his reading book.
Reads every word twice,
Although he reads a lot
He's really quite nice.
Robert with his reading book
Tripped on a tin
He wondered where on earth he was
Inside a bin.
Robert without his reading book
Really quite upset,
Wanted somethin' else to do
So he bought himself a pet.

Rachel Daniels (12)
Bishop Walsh School

THE BALLAD OF BARRY THE FISH

This is Barry, he's a fish
But you can't eat him in a dish
He swims about in the sea,
He's nothing like you or me.

There are many colours
For us to see
He swims in pairs
Two or three.

He camouflages
It's hard to describe
But to survive
He swims and hides.

He's not a predator
He's a prey
He could be eaten
Right here today.

Nick Jealous (13)
Bishop Walsh School

FEAR OF MICE!

Mice in my kitchen scare me to death,
They chase me around until I'm out of breath,
They have claws and a tail, their eyes they do stare.
I see their sharp teeth which will give me a scare.
They have little houses in the side of my wall
And I can't ever catch them because they're so small.
I jump on a table, I jump on a chair
I really do hate them so I'm always aware.
I think of diseases, I think of their fleas.
I reckon I'll catch them with one piece of cheese.
I see little bite marks, I smell them for miles.
I think of their faces with their evil smiles.
Then I think to myself, I have nothing to fear.
So I get down on my knees and let them come near.
I put down my hand and the mouse climbs on.
Then I think to myself, my fear has gone.

Catherine Taylor (13)
Bishop Walsh School

HUNGRY HAROLD HODGESON

Hungry Harold Hodgeson
The greediest kid in town
Plodin' down the road,
You'll hear his feet come down.
Eatin' several hot dogs
Like there's no tomorrow,
Gettin' really messy
Cutlery, ha, he don't need to borrow.

Hungry Harold Hodgeson
Hears an ice-cream van
Starts to jog after the truck
Boy you should 'a seen how he ran.
Not lookin' where he's going',
He fell down a manhole
And then he got stuck
He had to be prised out with a flag pole.

Hungry Harold Hodgeson
Now I think he knows
That when he's chasin' ice-cream
He'll be lookin' where he goes.
But now he's got a swellin'
Around his big fat belly.
So now he can't eat hot dogs
Or ice-cream and jelly.

Liam Mooney (12)
Bishop Walsh School

MARY WITH HER MOBILE

Mary with her mobile
Walking down the street
Not paying any attention
To the people she meets
Mary with her mobile
Thinking she is cool
When everyone just
Thinks she is a fool.

Mary with her mobile
Talks and walks across the road
Doesn't even care
About the Highway Code
Talking on her mobile
Doesn't hear a sound
Doesn't hear the workmen
Working underground.

Mary with her mobile
Fell down the hole
Got some cuts and grazes
When she landed on some coal
Mary with her mobile
What an ugly sight
When someone looked at her
They got an awful fright.

Mary with her mobile
Will she ever learn
To look where she is going
And to show us some concern?

Anastacia O'Donnell (12)
Bishop Walsh School

ROLLING THE ROLLERBLADES MISHAP RAP

Robin on his rollerblades
Rollin' down the road
Swerving round the people
Unt bumping a load.

Robin on his rollerblades
Rollin' through the traffic
Jumpin' over curbs
Unt make 'em panic.

Robin on his rollerblades
Snakin' about
Windin' through the people
In and out.

Robin on his rollerblades
Going through red
Hit by a lorry
Unt thinkin' he's dead.

Robin on his rollerblades
Lyin' on the road
Here comes the ambulance
To cart off the load.

Robin holding his rollerblades
Lyin' on his bed
Sad he can't go roller-blading
But glad he isn't dead.

Macius Grudzinski (12)
Bishop Walsh School

MOLLY WITH HER MOBILE

Molly with her mobile
Trying to look cool
Phoning all her mates up
Skipping off school.

Molly with her mobile
Saw someone she knew
Tried to do her hair up
In the window view.

Molly with her mobile
Too busy with the *flow*
Walked into a lamp post
Suffered a mighty blow.

Molly with her mummy now
In a hospital bed
A big crack in her mobile
A bandage 'round her head.

Molly with no mobile
Decided to go to school
Being a very good girl now
Had enough of being cool!

Nicola McMullan (12)
Bishop Walsh School

LUKE THE LADIES' MAN

Luke the ladies' man
Strutting up the hill,
Staring at the ladies
Thinking he's chill,
His real name's Gerard
But people call him Luke
Staring at the ladies
Reckoning he's 'ard.

Luke the ladies' man
Playing with his hair
Reckons he's a hard nut
Swearing at the mayor
Thinks the ladies love him
Thinks he's well cool
Says he's good at football
Never goes to school.

Luke the ladies' man
Hit by a punk
Can't go to school now
Thinks that he'll flunk
Limping down the pavement
Looking pretty dead
Walking like a zombie
A cut on the head.

Chris Budd (12)
Bishop Walsh School

FREDERICK AND HIS FOOTBALL

Frederick and his football
A-hoppin' down the street
Doesn't let the ball
Slip away from his feet.
Wearin' his T-shirt
With all his pride
Doesn't stop to think
Just carries on to glide.

Frederick and his football
A-boppin' down the road
Showin' off his skills
But lookin' like a toad.
Concentrating hardly
Trying his very best
Doesn't stop to notice
The traffic from the west.

Frederick and his football
Bouncin' down the lane
Doesn't stop to think
He's in trouble again.
Steps off the kerb
A big mistake
Doesn't see the cyclist
Which leg did he break.

Frederick with no football
Better off without
Next time he'll be lookin'
And listening' for a shout.

Daniel Lambe (13)
Bishop Walsh School

THE BALLAD OF JOHNNY

There was a boy called Johnny
Who was very sad
He was always alone
He only had a dad.

Johnny's mother died
When Johnny was only five
Johnny said to himself one day
'I wish my mother was still alive.'

Johnny's dad went out one night
And left Johnny all alone.
Johnny wandered to himself
'I wonder why he hasn't phoned?'

Johnny's dad came back the next day
With a very small lady
He woke up the next morning
To find at breakfast, her daughter Sadie.

Johnny's father married the lady
On a special day
He married her in Cyprus
On a beach called Coral Bay.

Johnny now had a mum and sister
He was very happy
He now had a new family
He was a very happy chappy.

Danielle McGuire (13)
Bishop Walsh School

DREAMING OF ALIENS

There once was a boy and his name was Mike,
But the problem was that Mike was very bright.
He became bored of everything and so went to bed
To rest his exceedingly overworked head.

He fell into a deep sleep and all became a whirl,
Then the very next minute, he was in a different world.
He stood still and saw a fantastic creature,
With oh! so many brilliant features.

He went over towards him to have a chat,
But unfortunately the alien was smelly and fat.
'Well I'll just follow him then, wherever he goes,'
Said Mike, 'This should be fun I suppose!'

The alien went off to a wrestling match
Mike hoped he'd watch the alien get scratched.
There was no action that Mike could see
Only two aliens as loving as could be.

The opponents stood there and complemented each other,
Just as if they were two caring brothers,
Mike said aloud, 'There is no action'
The aliens replied 'We shall turn you into something
That might catch your attraction.'

Mike awoke, out of bed he fell,
No longer Mike, now Michelle!

Tom Hyde (13)
Bishop Walsh School

HUNTING

My problem is unique,
Nobody knows it but me,
For what it is,
Is a matter of honour
And a tradition that I must now carry.

My father and his before him,
Have always hunted in these woods,
Making their first kill years before I have,
But a problem has risen in the face of more hunting
And that problem is known as people.

'It's not legal!' they say
And they really do mean it,
I daren't walk through town with a gun,
But I must keep tradition, if only this once
And make my first kill today.

I reach for the rifle,
I load it as well and sling it
Over my back. As I walk out the house
And into the night,
I wonder, 'What will I catch today?'

Joseph Young (13)
Bishop Walsh School

BACK IN THE PLAYGROUND SUNSHINE

Dreamed I was back in the playground sunshine
Where children run and play
Swings swinging, footballs flying and every child laughing.

There are swings swinging in the middle
A football pitch to the left
Small wooden fence all around
Small and new as I am, I fit straight in.

People are laughing,
People are running,
People are playing,
People are helping others,
They help you for anything at all.

The bigger people come to play
They play with anyone,
Heard a noise, time to go in
But never the less, there's next time still to come.

Amy Lee (12)
Bishop Walsh School

MY PHOBIA OF SPIDERS

When I hear the word nightmare,
I think of spiders.
Spiders are my worst nightmare
Their furry, black bodies make my skin crawl.
The way they scurry so fast across the floor,
Makes me want to run;
But in the opposite direction!
The fear I have when I see one spider,
Is the same as if I had seen twenty.
The same fluttery feeling comes to my stomach
And fills my body with cold pimples.
One little spider makes me scream as much as one big one.
As I watch the spider crawl over the surface,
I cover my face and squirm.

Sarah Burns (13)
Bishop Walsh School

THE SKY

I look up to the morning sky
To feel the warmth
Of the day go by.

The sky gets dark
The wind sets in
I pull a rag up to my chin.

I feel the cold
It's hurting now
I close my eyes.

Then curl up tight
I think to myself
That I might be in
The warmth of somewhere nice.

I start to shiver,
The moon light stops
It's all gone quiet.

It hurts no more
I am warm again
The light has gone
And taken me too.

Paul Farrelly (13)
Bishop Walsh School

MOVING HOUSE

One day my mum started packing
My dad parked a lorry outside
My big sister was running like mad
Although she looked extremely sad.

I walked down the hall to my room
I was in for a big surprise
Nothing was there
Not even the bed or the teddy bear.

I went downstairs to ask my mum
Where all my possessions had gone
But all she did was stare
And say we were going somewhere.

Now I was in the car
And I said 'Mum is it going to be far?'
She didn't answer, but I didn't have any cares
Because I saw my dad go past in the lorry
That said tables and chairs.

When we got there
I saw the beach
But it was bare
But I thought that was very rare.

When we got near a house
(Which was twice as big as our old one)
Then I was told that Friday afternoon
My parents came into a fortune.

Michael O'Brien (13)
Bishop Walsh School

JUNK FOOD

Choccy biccies, buttered toast,
Are the things you love the most!
On sweets and humbugs, you are glued,
You are stuck on all junk food.

Pancakes and syrup, get piled high,
Junk food's the only way you get by.
And when I ask for eating tips,
You only think of fish and chips!

And when you know we're in a hurry,
Your mind is switched to spicy curry
And where's the sense, for goodness sake -
In filling yourself with chocolate cake!

And do you think you're being good,
On stuffing your face with treacle pud?
Even too much raspberry jelly
Can give a girl, a big, round belly!

And you must stop, eating bacon fried,
Or you will end up fat and wide!
So you must give junk food a goodbye wave
And become a crazy diet slave!

Jenny Keitch (13)
Bishop Walsh School

THE NIGHT OF '81

Far away in Rotterdam,
Some Germans awaited Villa,
They were the favourites,
But a saviour elapsed beyond Jimmy Rimmer.
A young keeper,
Called Nigel Spink,
Came out for his debut,
But it looked as if the Villa defence was already on the brink.
He made some fine saves,
From Munich's crème de la Monde
They couldn't score from anywhere,
The Villa defence had formed a bond.
Time wore on,
Light grew dim,
As Munich pushed,
For that all elusive win.
A hero came through
His name was Peter Withe,
From Moreley's cross,
He slotted home a typical Withe goal.
We won the game,
Thanks to the hero,
We were the best in Europe,
But soon the hero signed for Wolves and soon hit zero.

Patrick Geary (13)
Bishop Walsh School

SHOW OFF SKATEBOARD SID

Show off skateboard Sid,
Skatin' in the rink,
Doin' all the tricks,
Pity he don't think.
People starin' at him,
Thinks he's so good,
Lucky he don't slip,
Some wish he would.
Show off skateboard Sid,
Doin' turns and twists,
Loops in the air,
This time he missed!
Fallin' to the ground,
Then a great big crack,
Ambulance is comin',
Broken arm and back.
Safety skateboard Sid,
Skatin' in the rink,
Doin' all the tricks,
But this time he thinks.
If he falls again,
He won't feel a thing,
His helmet and shin pads,
This time he'll bring.

Lisa Martin (12)
Bishop Walsh School

I HATE RAIN!

Dripping through the shelters
Thundering on your head
Slipping down your coat
You wish you'd stayed in bed!

It rumbles on your car,
Streaming down the panes
With such a loud annoying noise
So similar to a cane!

They say it's to do with nature;
But I think it's far beyond
A message from the heavens
Or a curse from tribe Zing Zong.

I think that you'll agree
It will happen at bad times
Whilst hanging out the washing
Or summer partying to Busta Rimes!

You've just got the barbecue started
Sausage, burger, kebabs and steak
When the clouds turn black and everyone sighs
You might as well chuck your food in the lake!

Whatever the reason good or bad
Rain's the biggest pain I've ever had!

Tonia Brown (13)
Bishop Walsh School

I Wish . . .

I wish I could go out to space
Up there in that beautiful place.
Oh I wish I could fly
High up in the sky
Where I would wander amongst the stars,
What is it like to live on Mars?

I wish I could go to the deep
Far below where the oceans sleep,
Where the sea monsters roam
In their dark murky home
Where mermaids swim free
So amazing to see.

I wish I could do all this
And live in harmony and bliss
But I'm only a lad
Though I'll grow up like my dad
And I'll meet the aliens and swim with the fish
But for now all I can do is to wish!

Philip Giannecchini (13)
Bishop Walsh School

Homework

Homework is a drag
That's when Mum starts to nag
Maths, English, Science, RE
When we'd rather be watching TV.

Worst of all it takes us ages,
Turning all those textbook pages
We pack our bags with our books
The whole class with grumpy looks.

'Get your homework diaries out, please'
The phrase that makes us sneeze
'I don't feel well, I think I've got the flu,'
We say when we hear what homework we've to do.

We know we have to do it,
Or else it's a detention from Mr Hewitt
So we get to the library just in time
And have it done by five to nine.

Daniel O'Sullivan (13)
Bishop Walsh School

CLAUSTROPHOBIA

Oh no, oh no, please get me out!
I'm going to start to scream out.
There's no space, no room, nor air,
Is there nobody outside there?

Please, I'm begging, open the door,
There's no space, I need more!
All of the walls are closing in,
My head has begun to whirl and spin.

I've started to panic, I need to get out,
Can't anyone hear me shout?
I keep on trying, this door won't open,
I'm positive that the lock has broken.

That's it, it's the end, I'm going to die,
I say to everyone farewell, goodbye,
Wait, what's that in the corner of the floor?
Hang on - whoops, it's the key for the door!

Lydia Mulkeen (13)
Bishop Walsh School

THE BALLAD OF RONALDO

He's been scoring goals
Ever since he was a young boy,
Just kicking a ball
Never picked up a toy.

A few years later
His family, still poor,
They needed more money
It was to come for sure.

He was only a teenager,
Still growing in age,
When the striker Ronaldo
Had made the front page.

He plays for his country
(And is now a grown man),
Still scoring goals
Whenever he can.

He has sponsorship deals
With companies a-many,
So his family now needs
Not another penny.

Aaron Condron (13)
Bishop Walsh School

THE BALLAD OF JOHN PAUL CHADWICK

This is the ballad of John Paul Chadwick
(Handsome face, gorgeous smile)
Always cheerful, forever happy
You can tell it's him from a mile.

At the age of eight, John decided
A journalist he wanted to be,
To be the best and very famous
A millionaire by forty-three.

He started on his road to fortune
By staying alert and working hard
By passing exams and showing promise
And always staying on his guard.

He climbed the ladder very quickly
Although some obstacles got in his way,
Like girls and cars and socialising,
Then he realised business came before play.

And now he's at University
And everything he touches turns to gold
He still works hard and is achieving
The plans he had when he was eight years old.

Helen Chadwick (13)
Bishop Walsh School

THE BALLAD OF ME ON SATURDAY MORNINGS

Oh I don't want to get up on Saturday,
I think it's completely unfair,
I'd much rather stay in my bed,
Next to my cuddly bear.

Oh I don't want to get up on Saturday,
I'd rather lie in my bed,
Don't they know that it's very important,
That I rest my weary head.

Oh I don't want to get up on Saturday,
I know my bedroom's a mess,
I ought to be bright and breezy,
Revising for Monday's maths test.

Oh I don't want to get up on Saturday,
I know the chores need to be done.
My sister shrieks 'Lucy get up,'
She's always spoiling my fun.

Oh I don't want to get up on Saturday,
I'd rather lie here and just doze.
My eyes are so weary, outside's so dreary,
Now Max is licking my nose.

Lucy Crough (13)
Bishop Walsh School

THE BALLAD OF ANNIE MCDUFF

Annie McDuff was a Scottish lass,
She was a stunner at five foot ten,
She had luscious blonde curls and big blue eyes
And she attracted all the young men.

She wanted to work in a zoo
Ever since the age of three
She even kept pet monkeys
Named Archibold and Lee.

One day the two monkeys escaped
And caused a rumpus in the town
They took sweeties from the sweet shop
And from the dress shop, a silky gown.

'What have you done?' her mother scowled,
Filled with contempt and anger.
That was fourteen years ago and now
She has a child called Tapanga.

She once went for an interview
To work in a reptile house,
She didn't like snakes or lizards,
So she worked with some bugs and a louse.

She now has been promoted,
To work with the monkeys instead,
She's filled with joy and laugher
And she's also happily wed.

James McFadzean (13)
Bishop Walsh School

THE BALLAD OF JON ALLEN

Struggling to be a superstar
A dream that's meant to be,
A dream not going anywhere
We'll have to wait and see.

He wants to be a rockstar
And make it to the top,
Travel all around the world
Keep going and never stop.

Gareth, Jim, Justin, Mark
And last, but not least, Jon,
They all belong to the band, 'The Trace'
They're aiming for number one.

To his fans he is incredible
He passes every test,
They go to all his concerts
They think he is the best.

Someday he's going to get there
And so are all the others,
I am so very proud of Jon,
Jon Allen, my big brother.

Jennifer Allen (13)
Bishop Walsh School

THE BALLAD OF JOHNNY COOL

Johnny was the most popular guy,
In the USA, Connecticut High,
Although still at school,
He thought he was cool.

His hair was jet black
And always slicked back
He used lots of gel
And my could you tell!

He looked in the mirror,
The sight made him quiver,
He dressed in a suit,
'Cos he thought it was cute!

He wore a bright tie,
Like a real macho guy,
The colours didn't matter,
As he thought he could flatter.

Sadly for him,
The girls thought him dim,
They laughed and they giggled,
Some whistled and wiggled;

'Dear Johnny,' they said,
'You've got such a big head
You act like a smoothy
And could star in a movie.'

'They think I'm a star!
I'm sure I'll go far,
Leo watch out!
Johnny Cool is about!'

Laura Morley (13)
Bishop Walsh School

PRINCE CHARMING

There was a young boy, about age fourteen,
Who was charming and witty and sweet,
About 5ft 4 and pretty lean
And generally indiscreet.

The girls had fallen head over heels
For this funny personality,
With lustrous eyes (it was totally unreal)
His smile drove them to insanity.

Then one day their friend appeared
To say hello to them all,
'You're a fat lard' a voice declared
The group was totally appalled.

From that day on, they began to question
Their friendship with Prince Charming
'Don't speak to him' was the best suggestion,
'His behaviour was simply alarming.'

Aimua Omoigui (13)
Bishop Walsh School

EVERYTHING BUT THE LAD

His eyes like chocolate daring but smart,
His smile so charming, it captures your heart,
His hair like velvet, tender to touch,
Even though he's small, we love him very much.
His muscles like steel, strong but kind
It's only when you meet him, you see what I find,
I think about him every hour of every day,
I love everything about him in every single way.

Kelly McGihon (13)
Bishop Walsh School

MY FRIEND

It was in reception,
Where we first met,
Looking after the gerbil,
The reception year's pet.

Remember the times,
That we spent together?
Those summers were long
They lasted forever.

And then there was sixth form,
Our final year,
Soon we would be choosing,
Our boring career.

But you said, 'No!
Let's have some fun!
We'll join up together
What do ya think, me son?'

Our business bloomed,
(Well it was a florist)
And for years we owned
A good profiting forest.

For years and years
We've been together,
Stuck with each other
For ever and ever!

Catherine Gagin (14)
Bishop Walsh School

GROWN UPS

Grown ups will bang you about
For doing nothing and saying nout
Will I be like that when I grow up?
I hope not.

They make you eat your greens,
Why? No child knows
They call you in at 8 o'clock
Even in the holidays.

They make you do your homework
When you want to watch TV
They make you tidy your room
But they won't take later
For an answer.

Now I'm a grown up now,
I'm no different to my parents
My kids think the same as I did,
I don't care, I'm a grown up.

Russell John Davies (13)
Bishop Walsh School

MIGHTY MOTH

More terrifying than the howling wolf
As it stalks its fated prey
Is the little bitty tiny moth
That eats my clothes away.

More deadly than the vampire bat
Which makes my blood run chill
Is the pea sized winged monster
As it moves in for the kill.

More unnatural than the gliding ghosts
That haunt our darkest dreams
Is the seemingly immortal moth
Dressed in browns and creams.

More powerful than all these horrors
As it ramraids past my eyes
Is this fearful lepidoptera
Of a microscopic size!

Sarah Devlin (13)
Bishop Walsh School

A BRIDGE TOO FAR

The tall, thin, pale man
Who smiles at the thought of pain
He sits and waits to torture people
Knowing they are helpless and under his power
With their mouths wedged open.
You lie back on the chair
And catch a whiff of the clinical smell
The light is flicked on, you are blinded
By the brightness in your eyes
And immediately you are under his power
A long thin metal instrument trespasses in your mouth
He calls out numbers 'One, two, three molars, one possible bridge'
This was one bridge too far for me!

Emma Flynn (13)
Bishop Walsh School

SCARED!

I'm scared of scary spiders,
Climbing up the wall.
I'm scared of big monsters,
Nearly 10 feet tall.

I'm scared of wriggly worms,
Crawling up my arm.
I'm scared of hot fire,
And a loud fire alarm.

I'm scared of the dark,
And what's lurking behind the door.
I'm scared of angry lions,
And their frightening roar.

I'm scared of being lost,
And not being found.
I'm scared of loud noises,
That make a horrible sound.

I'm scared of big rollercoasters,
Going upside-down.
I'm scared of my parents,
And their angry frown.

I'm scared of creepy-crawlies,
Crawling in my hair.
I'm scared of all the rides,
At the funfair.

I'm scared of high-up places,
What would happen if I fall?
I'm scared of flying in a plane,
1000 feet up tall.

But after all this has been said,
I'm not that scared at all.

Claire Suckling (13)
Bishop Walsh School

LOVE

Love is a wonderful thing
It can make your heart go *ping*
It can be your mother or your father,
It doesn't really matter
You'll still say the same.
When people fall in love
They thank the heavens above!
'It's great, it's fantastic'
They scream at the top of their voices.
My granddad and my nan
Fell in love whilst in his van
Then there's my mum and my dad
Well this is where it gets really bad.
It was on a summer's day
They were sitting on bales of hay
The sun was blazing
Their tongues were wagging
What more can I say?
I hope you agree with me,
Love, you can clearly see
Really is a wonderful thing
That makes your heart go *ping.*

Dominique Dwyer (13)
Bishop Walsh School

I RUN LIKE A CHEETAH . . .

I run like a cheetah
They say 'No one can beat ya!'
My long auburn mane catches the wind
I don't mind.
I'm gold and brown
And should really wear a crown.
Though a harness and a bit will do.
While them out there are freezing cold
I have a coat that's worth its weight in gold
For jumping and running and playing around
And for when I decide to roll on the ground.
While I can stand and watch the day go by
Others ask 'Where does time fly?'
I love to sit and laze all day
When home time comes it's time to play.
My best friend comes at half-past four
And we play till it's time to shut the stable door.
We can jump fences, run real fast
And love to trot down country paths.
I wish it could be summer,
I wish I could jump all day,
I wish I could open my stable door,
But I can't to my dismay!

Nicola Murrall (13)
Bishop Walsh School

THE BALLAD OF MUNICH 1958

It was a cold, cold February afternoon,
In Munich '58.
Some men were travelling back home again,
They didn't want to be late.

The Man Utd football team,
2-1 the score to report.
Harry Gregg, Bill Foulkes and Tommy Taylor,
The pride of British sport.

At 2pm they were ready to go,
The brave team boarded the plane,
The pilot tried, the engines roared,
But his attempts were all in vain.

At 2.34 they tried twice more,
They failed both times, a hefty blow,
The sky turned grey
And it began to snow.

With 3.03 the time they tried again,
The players didn't like the sound.
The plane took off, then dipped again
And the plane hit the ground.

Peter Mullins (13)
Bishop Walsh School

LOST

All alone on a dark, dark night,
Hoping that I won't get a fright.
Looking for my parents,
Where could they be?
Are they also looking for me?

A scary old man came down the street
He had shaggy clothes and dirty bare feet.
He searched through the dustbin
Looking for food,
But when he found none, went off in a mood.

I lay on a bench to get to sleep
But someone's car horn went beep, beep, beep,
Is it my parents?
I hope they're here,
No, they're not I realised with fear.

I awoke to bliss,
Being hugged and kissed,
My parents have found me at last,
How stupid I was to run away,
Forever I will regret that day!

Claire Keegan (12)
Bishop Walsh School

I HATE SPIDERS

I hate how spiders
Absail down walls.
I hate how spiders
Curl into balls.
I hate how spiders
Look black and hairy.
I hate how spiders
Look really scary.

I hate how spiders
Scurry around,
I hate how spiders
Bodies are round.
I hate how spiders
Look never weary.
I hate how spiders
Look very scary.

Samantha Goadby (13)
Bishop Walsh School

THE DOCTOR

The thing that scares me
Is the doctor's needle
You may think this is feeble,
Just to fear a doctor's needle.

Every time I visit the doctor,
I always spot her,
Getting a needle, ugh
I'd hate to be a doctor.

She comes towards me the doctor
Then once I stop her,
'No' is what I tell her.

Once I am free
And needle free
I think phew how lucky.

Then once back home
And when I'm alone
I say at least she
Wasn't a dentist!

Ciarán Mooney (13)
Bishop Walsh School

I HATE SPIDERS

I   really do dislike spiders.

H   airy and scary, they crawl around your room
A   ll eight legs crawl, crawl, crawl
T   hey taunt me day and night
E   verybody hates spiders, nearly everyone does, don't they?

S   pider, spider, crawling up the wall
P   lease don't hurt me I am only small
I   f you don't get out my room you're gonna
D   ie, die, die,
E   gg head spiders, jumping spiders
R   ed, red spiders, blue, blue spiders I hate them all
S   entry I stand guarding my room from spiders.

Gerard Kelly (13)
Bishop Walsh School

BACK IN THE PLAYGROUND SUNSHINE

I dreamed the sun was shining down on me, yes,
I was dreaming the sun was shining down on me,
No rain, no wind, just the sun shining down on me.

My first day of school but the sun was still shining
Down on me, I said shining down on me, playing in water,
Playing in sand there's nothing much we could do but I
Say the sun is shining down on me.

Don't know what happened that day but the sun
Was shining down on me, on me, that's what I say.

Fiona Fleming (12)
Bishop Walsh School

CLAUSTROPHOBIA

Being locked in is my worst nightmare,
I just can't bear it.
It is a fear that has given me the title
'Claustrophobic.'
Being confined is a terror,
A real trepidation,
But when I'm enclosed
I cannot stop this apprehension.
My heart begins to beat,
Pulse starts to rise,
I can't help but panic,
Is that wise?
I get really hot,
I almost fry,
I begin to feel tears,
I want to cry.
I start to sweat, I can't breathe,
I'm paranoid and I shiver,
I try to get out. I hit the wall,
I soon become a quiver.
'Is there anybody out there?'
It goes quiet and I try to hear.
Forget spiders or heights
This is my worst fear.

Sam Sparrow (13)
Bishop Walsh School

SNAILS

They disrupt everything!
I can quite happily be in the garden
And then my mum will turn to me
And see the colour from me drain,
The look on her face is oh so plain,
'Oh damn she's seen a snail again.'

I spotted it among the rocks,
So my drink I quickly dropped
But before it reached the floor, I screamed
'Oh gross, I bet there's loads more'

I ran to my mother,
But she was too near the frightful thing,
So my very own body I began to fling
I tied myself up in knots
I began to sweat though I was not hot.

It was as though my senses had been heightened
And that made me ten times more frightened,
It was as if I could hear them calling
'Michelle, Michelle, we're coming, we're crawling.'

But I'll get my revenge one day
I'll cover them with salt and look away
As they pop and they whiz
And they bubble and they fizz
Without batting the lid of an eye
I will easily be able to say goodbye.

Michelle Avery (13)
Bishop Walsh School

HEIGHTS

When I'm on a fairground ride
Or looking over a building side,
I want to hesitate,
As I think I'm going to faint.

As I ascend up a tower,
I'd rather be a flower
As on the ground I would see,
Everyone from you to me.

When I'm in the air,
The wind blows my hair,
My knees begin to shake
As I think they're going to break.

I feel so sick, I really do,
As I think I'm going to spew
I feel so paralysed,
From my feet, up to my eyes.

Up high I go no more
As I think I'm going to fall
On the ground, I have a place
Rather than the dizzy heights of space.

Emma McAuley (13)
Bishop Walsh School

I HATE RATS

I just can't help it, I can't stand rats
I don't mind snakes and I don't mind bats,
They're unhygienic with fleas and germs
Their tails are long, like slithering worms.

They feed on food from the night before
All sorts of rubbish, old chicken and more,
They live in sewers and can do as they please
If you get too close, you'll catch a disease.

They brought in the plague, three centuries ago,
On the boat, then the docks, then onto Soho,
In London the disease spread like fast running water
From father to son, to mother to daughter.

Most furry creatures fill us with delight,
Apart from rats, they just give us a fright,
They're in all the horror movies, ready to scare
Their beady eyes and squeaking is just too much to bear.

Yet we all find squirrels so cute and sweet
But if you take off their tail, you're in for a treat,
Shave off their long bushy tails and what do you find?
They're rats after all, not cute, sweet or kind.

So give me spiders and snakes any day
Even flying insects I think are OK.
But there's something about rats I just don't like
If I come across one, I'll be taking a hike!

Emma Lines (13)
Bishop Walsh School

THE BOTTOM OF THE SEA

There is one thing that really scares me,
I won't go near it at all,
I'm scared of the bottom of the sea,
Even if the water's ten feet tall.

You never know what's down there,
Under the deep, dark waves,
Big monsters in their lairs,
Sharks hiding in big, dark caves.

I never put my feet on the seabed,
In case something makes a grab at me,
I don't want to be the one who is fed,
To the 'thing' at the bottom of the sea.

Sarah Saveker (13)
Bishop Walsh School

NEEDLES

What should I do?
There's no way out!
I block my thoughts out, but still there's doubt,
About this pain which I must take to keep me healthy,
Is this my fate?
The needle directed into my arm,
There is no more pain, the doubt has gone.
But still there's always a next time for this pain,
So paranoia will come again.

Emile Ngene (13)
Bishop Walsh School

Lost!

I once was lost among the crowd,
I started to call out loud.
Mom! Mom! Mom! Mom!
But alas she was gone.

I looked around and ran away,
My stomach turned, I began to sway.
Mom! Mom! Mom! Mom!
But alas she was gone.

I started to think I'd never be found,
No one seemed to care, as I looked around,
Mom! Mom! Mom! Mom!
But alas, she was gone.

I sat down in just one place,
And I saw the beautiful face of,
Mom! Mom! Mom! Mom!

Beaumont Hadley (13)
Bishop Walsh School

The Tragic Baby

She once was a child so sweet and mild,
Laying in her cradle thinking of her mother so mild,
As she lay there thinking of you,
She wondered what on earth she could do,
As her life suddenly flew by,
She decided to give you one last kiss goodbye.

Sarah Szymmelpfennig (12)
Britannia High School

GHOSTS OF A SCHOOL CHILD

(Dedicated to Carly-Jo, for being a great friend)

She wanders lonely through the walls,
Her voice cries out, echoing throughout the halls,
The tears rolling down her cheeks,
Not one friend has she had, although she seeks.
Her wispy hair drapes over her face,
Her face so washed out, she can't keep up the pace,
Night after night, spending time alone,
She's had enough, no ringing of a phone.
She once used to be a school child,
Then to heaven someone dialed,
The day before she bought a coat, just to blend,
As all she longed for, was just one friend.

Stacey Marshall (12)
Britannia High School

A BAD NIGHT

When I go to bed tonight
I know I'm in for a nasty fright.
'Cause I stayed up to see a bloodthirsty movie
Where somebody's brain was splattered on the duvet.
And now I lie in bed awake
And in my mind I see a snake.
I look up, towards the ceiling
And get a sudden sinking feeling.
When I wake up in the morning
I'm still tired and am yawning.

Ben Young (12)
Britannia High School

ALIENS FROM OUTER SPACE

Aliens from outer space,
I wish I could go to that place.
Or maybe they will live with me,
Or what about under the sea?
Aliens invent exciting new things,
Or maybe they will invent some flying wings.
I hope they will teach me a new language,
Or maybe make a new sandwich.
Perhaps they'll be able to change shape
And clear away all the waste.
Perhaps they'll make our wishes come true,
Or play hide and seek and say *boo!*
Maybe they will take over the world
And make beautiful rings, with beautiful pearls.

Charlotte Moseley (12)
Britannia High School

HOMEWORK

My homework was a verse to write,
I thought about it half the night.
I looked through a book for inspiration,
But it was full of useless information.
I played with my dog, I thought it might help,
All it did was bark and yelp.
I asked my mom to do it for me,
I cannot tell you what she called me.
All the while I ate my tea,
I kept on thinking God, why me?
Finally I had an idea
And here it is written right here.

Harry Dean (12)
Britannia High School

My Mum

(This poem is dedicated to my mum)

When God was making mothers
As far as I can see,
He spent a lot of time on one
And saved that one for me.
He made a perfect woman
Compassionate and kind,
With more affection
Than you could hope to find.
He gave this lovely lady
A heart of solid gold
And after he had finished
He must have broken the mould.

Zoe Wood (12)
Britannia High School

My Lover

I met him in the park
While I was walking in the dark.
I have never seen anyone as handsome as he,
For he is the one that got married to me.
I will never forget him that's what I said
As he was lying on his deathbed.
I will treasure his picture
For that is what will remind me of the love I once had.
But as I lie awake at night
Things are going round in my head,
About my lover that is now dead.

Adelle Breakwell (12)
Britannia High School

HORROR FILMS

Horror films
Can be scary.
Werewolves are so wary
Murderers stalk and slice
When they think it's very nice.
Vampires sink teeth in neck
Ghosts coming from a shipwreck.
Zombies risen from graves
Demons making people slaves.
I watch a horror film
I'm so scared.
But if there's one behind me . . .
Who cares!
It's just a horror film
Ha! Ha! Ha!

Thomas Rutter (11)
Britannia High School

TWO OF MY BEST FRIENDS

My mom and dad are my
Best friends,
I know our love will never
End,
I know a boy who hates
His mom,
Why, oh why! This is very
Dumb.
I couldn't hate someone
This close to my heart
Even though they are apart.

Kirsty Jane Phipps (12)
Britannia High School

THE TRAGIC BOY

I once knew a boy,
As gentle as could be,
No one I knew,
Could be as handsome as he.

As he drove to the park,
In pitch-black dark,
He never came home,
So I was alone.

Then I knew,
What had happened to him,
I knew it was suicide
Because his life was so dim.

As I lay in bed,
Starting to cry,
His last kiss,
Was a kiss *goodbye.*

Charlene Hadley (12)
Britannia High School

THE TITANIC

I like the Titanic
But it was a big panic
When she goes down
She won't even be worth a pound.
When the lights go out
Fights will break out
Now she's gone down,
2,200 souls have also gone down.

Karl McGilligan (11)
Britannia High School

I WANT YOU TO KNOW . . .
(Dedicated to Adam Hodgetts, 11CF)

I want you to know how much I love you.
I want you to know what I'd do to be with you.
I want you to know I've missed seeing you.
I want you to know I hope we could be together.
I want you to know I really love you.
But last of all I want you to know
I promise I will be there,
To care, to hold you, to love you
And to be there when you need me.
I want, I want, I want you to love me
Like I love you and understand the way I feel about you.

Jennifer Baker (12)
Britannia High School

FUTURE VOICES

F or your home the Millennium Dome
U nder water life has grown
T o people like you and me
U pside down under and over flying is a breeze
R obots have invaded our homes
E veryone uses telepathy

V oices have been forgotten
O ver under upside down
I s this the Earth or is it the moon?
C hocolate milk comes out of taps
E veryone is big and fat
S paceships are used like cars.

Michelle Lavender (11)
Britannia High School

Just Dream

One has a dream
That the world will be a better place
Beautiful creatures and animals too.

One has a dream
That robots will take over the world.
But the only problem is
The teachers will have them all!

One has a dream of dogs, cats,
They are all so beautiful.
They bring you happiness, joy and laughter.

One has a dream
Of floating above the clouds,
Floating and floating away
I'm in heaven!

Sinead Langan (12)
Britannia High School

The Haunted Mill

Never go down to the haunted mill
I have been to the haunted mill
If you go in the haunted mill
You may not ever come out.

There is a ghost in the mill
That's what everybody says
In the crusher it says
But he will never come out.

David Banner (11)
Britannia High School

THE SPOOKS

Is this a dream, or is it not?
Something's in the baby's cot.
Downstairs, the rocking chair,
Is someone sitting there?
Squeaking floorboards,
Moving cupboards,
Is my home a haunted house
Or is it just a little mouse?
Outside my room is something moving?
I need something that is soothing.
Wait, what's that, it's just raining
Listen, the piano, is it playing?
All these things are scaring me,
I need to find out, look and see.

I take one step,
To the door I crept.
It's so dark, I'm all alone.
Oh no there goes the phone!
Over I go to the ringing,
All I hear is someone singing.
Is someone tricking me?
The door, it's locked, I need a key.
Oh no, I hear a painful scream!
Boy, I wish I had a team!

Leeanne Nichole Smith (13)
Britannia High School

FUTURE VOICES

F uture voices are coming
U s wearing strange clothes
T he new activities are coming out
U s seeing light coming our way
R eminding people to have a break
E verybody saying 'Look!'

V oices singing
O ur parents saying 'Bye' before we go
I n the street children riding on their bikes
C hildren are happy
E very star shining in the sky

Lisa Field (11)
Britannia High School

FUTURE VOICES

F uture voices are coming to town
U nless I hear voices coming
T he light of the sun is very hot
U ntil I hear different voices I won't believe
R obot teachers are coming to town
E veryone changes

V oices of different people are coming near
O ut of fashion computers go
I nto strange streets I will go
C ome on we're going on an adventure
E veryone coming on a new adventure
S o many children like new adventures.

Natalie Revitt (11)
Britannia High School

FUTURE VOICES

F lying away in the air
  Future voices
U nder water little people live
  Future voices
T alking animals, won't that be great?
  Future voices
U p we go into space
  Future voices
R obots can do our work and homework
  Future voices
E ven money can grow on trees
  Future voices

V ery big aliens taking over the world.
  Future voices
O n the moon we breath
  Future voices
I n the Millennium Dome we live
  Future voices
C ould zombies be our next-door neighbours?
  Future voices
E very human will change shape
  Future voices
S till it will be a great world.

Amy Salt (11)
Britannia High School

WHILE YOU WERE SLEEPING
(Dedicated to Stacey Marshell)

While you were sleeping, the minutes ticked by,
Hour after hour, I watched you die,
Surely I knew my heart would break,
How could you cause me so much heartache?
While you were sleeping I kissed your cheek,
To see you so fragile and weak,
My eyes filled with tears,
With you gone how would I face my fears?
I went to walk away, my heart told me I had to stay,
While you were sleeping the minutes ticked by,
Hour after hour, I watched you die,
Hours on end I asked myself why?
I gave you one final kiss to say goodbye.

Emma Sutton (12)
Britannia High School

THE SWIMMING BATHS

The smooth strokes of the waves,
The splash of disturbance,
Where am I?
The smoothness of the surface,
The floating of the bubbles,
Where am I?
The men that stand tall with long bare legs,
Who are ready to help the poor and helpless,
Where am I?
The hotness of the showers
And the cubicles so small,
Where am I?

Samantha Davenport (13)
Britannia High School

MY POEM

Autumn is here,
Leaves start to fall,
Sitting in the garden,
Then Mom starts to call.

'Don't go out there,' says Mom,
'You'll catch a cold,
Now stay inside,
Like you've been told.'

Leaves start falling,
One by one,
'I'm going to work now,' says Dad,
'Be good while I'm gone.'

Lisa Hyde (12)
Britannia High School

HOLIDAYS

My mom and dad my brother and I
Went to Majorca but we had to fly.

When I got there the sun was hot
So me and my brother played a lot.

We played on the beach
We played in the sea.

But after a week of all this fun
We had to say goodbye to the sun.

My mom and dad my brother and I
All sat on the plane and waved goodbye.

Goodbye!

Natalie Adlam (11)
Britannia High School

NEW SCHOOL

I can't wait till tomorrow
My new school is what I mean
Mom says I'll look smart
Posh and very clean.

Right I'm ready for school
Spruced up and looking my best
I'll have to do pages of writing
I hope not a test.

I'm walking into the gates now
Looking very shy
Mom's in our car now
Waving me goodbye.

The bell has just gone now
Ring! Ring! Ring!
We have music first of all
Oh no, I'm not in the mood to sing!

Going out to break now
Liking my new school very much
I'm proud of my work today
I must have a magic touch.

It's lesson time now
We're all writing away
Hoping to get it all done
Before the end of the day.

It's home time now
Time to see my dad
He'll be glad to see me
No, I haven't been bad!

Rachael Kennedy (11)
Britannia High School

IN THE LAND OF THE KUNG FU FIGHTERS

In the land of the kung fu fighters
The people are terrible biters
They never have a party
That is very, very hearty.
What a clever lot of fighters.

In the land of the kung fu fighters
The people are always playing with lighters
They never start fires
Or ever have choirs.
What a spiteful lot of fighters.

In the land of the kung fu fighters
You never see them playing with mitres
But thousands of swords
Each tied up with cords.
What a peaceful lot of fighters.

Christopher Nock (12)
Britannia High School

ODE TO THE REDS

The first goal goes into the net,
Am I going to win that bet?
A good swift move,
Finished off by the Frenchman: Detrouve.
The crowd jumps up and starts to roar,
Who said that the game was a boring draw?
The ref blows the whistle for half-time,
The Reds' passing is certainly sublime.
Come full-time we'll be dancing all the way home,
Next week in Europe, we'll be off to Rome.

Parminder Mann (13)
Britannia High School

LIFE'S NOT THE RAINBOW YOU THOUGHT IT WAS

People take life for granted,
Not me.
I take life seriously,
You see.

You always say tomorrow,
Not me.
I always say yesterday,
You see.

Others watch television,
Not me.
I love to read books instead,
You see.
That's where we're
Different.

Dominique T Homer (12)
Britannia High School

THE DOVE

I looked up to the sky above
And saw a beautiful dove.
It flew so gracefully
So delicate in the sky.

Its feathers were pure white
That made it fly like a kite.
Miles and miles it can go
To a land where nobody goes.

Emma Deeming (11)
Britannia High School

NAN

There was always something special,
About the nan I used to have,
Some of the things she used to say and do,
Remembering my domino games with her,
The gowns she wore,
Cigarettes she'd smoke,
Always going on about Grandad,
He was a nice bloke.
Now when the moon is full and I'm sad,
She will sit with me and comfort me,
Hours we will spend,
She is one of my best friends,
It's sad her life did end,
She drifted in the sky,
As I waved a sorrowful goodbye.

Lisa Rock (12)
Britannia High School

MR KINGFISHER

As Mr Kingfisher passes by down the river towards the sea,
Fisherman say, 'Hello, goodbye' as Master
Kingfisher passes by gracefully around the river bends.
There's flashes of orange and blue which looks like
The sun beaming on the water,
But as you see the large beak you know exactly who it is.
It starts to rain so Mr Kingfisher decides to hide away
Under the trees and leaves ready to eat food yet again.

Michael Britton (14)
Britannia High School

UFO POEM

Walking through the park with my dog,
A spaceship beamed me up to the planet Zog
I looked all around,
Then I heard a sound,
A crashing, banging from behind a log.

A monster came up from under the ground
All I could feel was my heart going pound.
My feet felt stuck to the floor,
Then I saw a shining door
And I jumped in the spaceship with my hound.

I found the controls and we flew away,
I got back to Earth and it was the same day
It was very strange, my trip to Zog,
The only one who knows is my dog
But it's good to be home, that's what I say.

Matthew Kenny (11)
Britannia High School

WHEN I . . .

When I grow up I want to be a deep sea diver.
When I grow up I want to be a truck driver.
When I grow up I want to be the queen surrounded by all her jewels
And then one day my mom she said 'Don't be silly our little Milly,
When you grow up all big and tall, you'll be the best of all.'

Leila-Jayne Holland (11)
Britannia High School

TRAIN CRASH 1999
(A tribute to those who died)

A slow and silent search began,
Biggest tragedy in the history of man.
Grieving relatives awaited news,
Thought they could get away by having booze.
Searching through ash and twisted metal,
Thinking of dying, driving you mental.
The lights went out and the carriage seemed to catch fire,
It was getting hot, the flames were getting higher and higher.
I thought I was going to die,
Leaving my family to mourn and cry,
Until I saw the firefighter.
I noticed it was getting lighter,
I survived
But what about those who died?

Manjit Kaur (13)
Britannia High School

GHOST FEAR

In the wee small hours of the night
I awoke with such a fright.
Was there a ghost
At the bottom of my bed
Or was it just inside my head?
Then it disappeared out of sight
Into the blackness of the night.

Emma Clift (11)
Britannia High School

MY IDEAL SUNDAY DINNER

My ideal Sunday dinner would be
lots of cakes and a nice cup of tea,
And then, just to get rid of the taste
a few chocolate buttons and strawberry paste.

Instead of the peas, I would put in their place
some little green sweeties with a sour tangy taste.

Instead of some meat, I would put there instead
a big piece of fudge and a lot of flavoured bread,
And then comes the end and just to top it all up
a large strawberry sundae, in a large glass cup.

Rachel Salt (13)
Britannia High School

LIFE

Life is an opportunity, take it,
Life is a risk, risk it,
Life is a task, complete it,
Life is a lesson, learn it.

Life is a faith, believe in it,
Life is a struggle, accept it,
Life is a dream, fulfil it,
Live life for the moment,
This is not a rehearsal.

Sayna Ahmad (13)
Britannia High School

DREAMS

I woke up in a hot sweat,
The dream lingered in my mind,
It was unbelievable, horrifying, mysterious.
I walked into the bathroom,
Shivering in the dark,
In fear of what was behind.
As the chilling water splashed against my face,
Bang! Went the door, suddenly Mom strolled in.
Phew! Thank God it wasn't a ghost or a ghoul
Or any kind of monster for that matter.
'What's the matter dear?' she surprisingly asked.
I remained still and silent,
Who would believe me?
Still the dream lingered on in my mind.
'Nothing!' I replied sharply and
I walked through the spooky corridor.
I climbed back into bed,
Wondering what would happen next?

Sarah Holsey (11)
Britannia High School

WHAT I WANT FOR CHRISTMAS

I can't wait till Christmas morn,
Where I will be up at the crack of dawn.
I open all my presents and get a big surprise,
I found what I wanted hidden right inside.

Melissa Bastable
Britannia High School

BAD MOOD

This kid's annoying, he gets on my nerves,
So he's going to get what he deserves.
I'm in a very bad mood.

Got my fists clenched, ready for a fight,
Going to hit him when the time is right.
I'm in a very bad mood.

I'm right by him by o' heck,
The teacher's breathing down my neck.
I'm in a very bad mood.

Pulled up my fist, hit him round the eye,
I'll act as though I was just passing by.
I'm in a very bad mood.

Oh, oh I've been spotted by the head,
'It wasn't me,' is what I said.
I'm in a very bad mood.

I'm in detention, it's so sad,
I suppose it's what you get for being bad.
I'm in a *really* bad mood.

Adam Mole (13)
Britannia High School

MY LITTLE BROTHER

My little brother is a pest,
He likes to think he is the best,
He's ten years old but acts like four,
When he tries to annoy you he is hard to ignore,
When I do something wrong he tells my mother,
But after all he is my brother.

Shema Islam (13)
Britannia High School

MY FAMILY

My family,
My mam's a full-time cleaner,
That's all she ever does.
My dad's a human dustbin, be careful,
He'll eat the lot!
My sister's in the 'growing stage',
Better left alone.
My younger sister Becky is rather
Picky when it comes to food.
She'd rather have fish and chips
Or else she's in a mood.
My other sister Charlotte is the hardest
Four year old I know.
'Hand it over or else!'
Now you know my family,
Stay well clear.
My dad will have you in, downing a pint of beer!

Claire Duckers (12)
Darlaston Community School

MY HOUSE

My house is a terrible place to be,
Sometimes with my brother singing stupid rhymes,
My mom moaning all through the day,
Then there's my dad shouting at me for everything I say.
It's one of those times you wanna hide away and never
see the light of day.
Then you get this splitting headache which is really a pain,
Then you suddenly think you've gone *insane!*

Katie Owen (12)
Darlaston Community School

FAMILY LIFE

Family life, well what can I say?
Fights and scraps from day to day.
I'd describe my mom as a tape recorder,
'Tidy up your room,' she'd order.
Then there's my brother. What about him?
He's our human food dustbin!
And my sister squeaking like a mouse,
While she runs like a wild thing all around the house.
Oh yes, my dad. How could I leave him out?
When he's around, I don't even dare to mess about.

The part about my mom
I'd better take back,
Or I'll be finding myself
Getting a very hard smack.

Adell Givans (12)
Darlaston Community School

THINGS I LIKE

H   ayley likes the new Harry Potter books.
A   n eight mile walk is good for Hayley.
Y   ellow is my favourite colour.
L   ilac is the colour of my mom and dad's car.
E   gg is Hayley's horrible food.
Y   vonne is the best neighbour in the street.

P   izza and chips is what Hayley likes.
A   nimals are Hayley's favourite.
G   ary Glitter is Hayley's worst singer.
E   mma is Hayley's friend.

Hayley Page (12)
Darlaston Community School

BABIES, BABIES, BABIES

They moan and groan,
They do each day, they have each day for years.
I'm on my own,
I'm always bored,
I'm always crying tears,
I have no one that I can play with,
I reckon I'm a fool
Because every kid has a brother or sister at
my secondary school.
They're hanging out with each other,
they're having loads of fun,
But when will it be my turn? I'll go and ask Mom.
'Mom I want a baby.'
'Wait until you're eighteen.'
'No I'm on about you silly.'
'Me? No way.'
'You're totally mean.'

I know I'll go ask my dad, he'll say yes for sure,
I'm so sure he will say yes I reckon he wants more,
One or two or even four, great score.
'Dad I want a baby.'
'Wait until you're twenty.'
'No you silly, I know you will have plenty.'
'I have enough with you dear,
You're totally silly and wild
So I don't think that me or your mom could cope
with another child.'

'Please oh please, oh please Dad.'
'We're not having another baby, that's the rule.'
'Oh Dad don't be so cruel.'
So I don't have a sister,
So I don't have a brother,
But when it comes to family we always have each other.

Leanne Gibbs (13)
Darlaston Community School

FAMILY LIFE

Family life is really cool, sometimes I break every rule!
Playing my music really loud, banging the wall, jumping around.

Then my big sister shouts up the stairs, 'Shut the hell up
I can't hear myself think.'
I turn off my radio and shout back down,
'No I won't, anyway I think you stink.'

Then the baby starts to cry, my sister then says,
'I'd rather die!'

Then it starts to rain, Mom comes rushing in the house,
'Aaggh' I scream 'where's my pet mouse?'

He's wandered off down the stairs,
Round the house and under the chairs.
Then finally I found him in the baby's hands wrapped
Up in bunches of elastic bands.
So I take him off her and try to get him out,
Thank goodness he's alive,
Unlike my sister who is dead,
But Mom's already smacked her and sent her off to bed.

Leanne Potter (12)
Darlaston Community School

MY FAMILY LIFE

My dad's always groaning,
My mum's always moaning.
My sister she's just lost the plot,
My baby brother's crying in his cot.
Then at last they all go quiet,
I sit down on the sofa for a while,
Then I start to go berserk
My brother's scribbled on my work,
I cried out, 'Mum,'
That was so dumb.
She's come upstairs and slapped his bum,
Now my brother's gone to sleep,
Without a cry, without a weep,
And now I'm in a very deep sleep.

Zara Khalid
Darlaston Community School

JUST ME

Mom, Dad and three
It's never just me.
I always seemed to be surrounded,
Always crowded.

I dream one day
In the middle of May
To sit under a tree,
Just me!

I have two sisters,
I never miss them.
I have a dad
He always acts mad.

And then there's my mom,
She always talks on and on.
One day it will just be me
You'll see!

Sarah Osborne (12)
Darlaston Community School

MY SISTER

Family life isn't much fun,
I guess the same applies for everyone.
I hate it I really do,
I can't do things normal kids do.
You wanna know why?
Well I guess you do.
I have to baby-sit my sister
Who really isn't that cute!
I have to do it every night
Which really is a fright.
'I can't believe it' that's the saying.
I can't go dancing, prancing and playing.
Can someone help me? Please do.
I can't help saying, do I really have to!

Nikki Fitzmaurice (12)
Darlaston Community School

A POEM ABOUT FAMILY LIFE

Family life is all I've got,
My dad sits in the chair and is beginning to rot,
He's a couch potato can't you see?
All he watches is sport on TV,
He only stirs when he has his tea,
He likes fish and chips just like me.

My mom has a job, it's only part-time,
She works in the evening from five till nine.

And last of all there is me, the youngest of the clan,
My nickname's Lanky Larry,
But my real name is Sam.

I just go to school and try to learn a lot,
Family life's pretty good really
And that's all I've got.

Samantha Leckie (13)
Darlaston Community School

MY SUMMERTIME

When it is sunny I drink lemonade
And eat an ice-cream in the shade,
Sit under the tree, my tree, my drink nice and cool
And then I jump into the swimming pool,
I splash and splash acting the fool,
But then when it got too cool,
I got out of the pool.

Krystle Larkin (12)
Darlaston Community School

I'M THE OLDEST IN MY HOUSE

I'm the oldest in my house,
People say I sound like the tiniest mouse,
I will admit I'm sometimes shy.
My younger brother's always asking why?
I shout in a mood 'I don't know.'
Then to see him after that you'd think wow!
It's like he turns into a monster,
He'll grab my hair
And kicks my leg,
I say 'I beg.'
He shouts and bawls,
He drives my mom up all the walls (literally).

My sister always plays with dolls,
She seems so sweet.
Touch her dolls and the real her you'll meet,
She'll grab you, kick you, bite you,
She'll do it until you say 'Boo hoo.'

My mom is so sweet and nice,
Her favourite meal's anything with rice.
Even though she rules,
She is always very cool.
She buys me things,
Including rings.
Along with Dad she's my mate!
So you see we are the nicest
Adams Family!

Jennifer Spence (12)
Darlaston Community School

TICK-TOCK

Tick-tock the clock's ticking.
I'm bored.
Soon after my brother comes in
'What ya looking at?'
I answer 'That's the nicest thing you ever said.'

Tick-tock the clock's ticking.
Mum and Dad come in. 'Put the kettle on love'
They both say.
I reply, 'Hard day at work then?'
They both say, 'A very hard day at work love.'

Tick-tock the clock's ticking.
The cats miaow to come in.
They look at me as if to say, 'Where's my food?'
I reply, 'Ready for you two to eat.'

Tick-tock the clock's ticking.
I'm writing my day in my diary.
The last words come out just before my pen runs out.
This is my family in . . .

Elisha Thorpe (12)
Darlaston Community School

BEDTIME FEEL

I was tired and sleepy as I carried myself to bed,
As I puffed up my pillow and lay down my head.
As I pulled over my duvet and wrapped up warm,
Please let me stay like this until the day does dawn.

Jenny Dickson (11)
Darlaston Community School

DANCE OF THE DOLPHINS

Slow, slow, quick quick, slow,
Ride the waves,
And here we go.

Quick, quick, leap up high,
Arch your back,
It's time to fly!

Fly, fly, puff and blow,
Blow some bubbles,
In a row.

Puff, puff, waltz and spin,
Shake your tail,
Flick your fin.

Slow, slow, quick quick, slow,
Take a partner,
Dive down low.

Quick, quick, slow slow, quick,
Listen carefully,
That's the trick!

Stacey Watson (11)
Darlaston Community School

NAME POEM, DONNA HAWKINS

D   ogs I have one, his name is Max.
O   range squash I hate, but I love blackcurrant.
N   aughty I am never.
N   ice I am and I am kind.
A   lex is one of my step-brothers, Chris is the other.

H   olidaying in Wales I love.
A   ll my schoolwork I like.
W   ales and dolphins are nice.
K   elly is one of my friends.
I   have eight brothers and a step-sister.
N   ieces I have none.
S   tacey is my step-sister, she is okay to be with.

Donna Hawkins (11)
Darlaston Community School

MY FAMILY

Dad's not home yet,
Mom's having a fit,
My brother's doodling on the wall
With his Crayola kit.

Dad's come home now,
Over an hour late,
Mom's finished the tea,
Mmm! This tastes great!

It's time to go to bed now,
Up the stairs I go,
Sometimes I think I'm the only
Sane one I know!

Roxanne Webster (12)
Darlaston Community School

LIKES AND DISLIKES

Likes

Some of the things I like are:
Plump purple-pink plums
because every bite melts in my mouth.
The mouth-watering smell of fresh cake
because I can look forward to pudding.
But, what I like most of all is
the bright, white light of the moon on a winter's night
because it helps me get to sleep.

Dislikes

Some of the things I hate are:
Big, hairy, scary spiders
because they send shivers up my spine.
Yucky, green, smelly spinach
because it makes me feel sick.
But, what I hate most of all is
hearing the Spice Girls sing
because it sounds worse than a cat being strangled.

Rikki Stone (11)
Darlaston Community School

MILLENNIUM ANTS

There once was a group of tiny ants,
They lived in a pair of crusty pants.

They moved their home
To the Millennium Dome
Where they wriggled, farted and danced.

Tom Berry (13)
Heathfield Foundation High School

CHRISTMAS DAY

We get up early morning
To open all our presents,
To find the things we wanted
And the things we don't.

My sister wanted a Barbie doll
But she got a Sindy.
I got a mobile phone
And everyone had better ring me.

At last it's time for dinner,
All that turkey, veg and spuds
And after that it's pudding time,
Mince pies and Christmas puds.

Now that the day is nearly over,
All the presents have been opened
And the night is nearly dead,
Hopefully this time next year I'll be in *bed*.

Lee Shaw (13)
Heathfield Foundation High School

CHRISTMAS MORNING

I woke up early Christmas morning
I could hardly see,
And there was my sack full in front of me.

I jumped out of bed,
Nearly fell on the floor,
Ran down the stairs and opened the door.

I saw it was snowing,
I ran back in,
I ran back upstairs and tucked myself in.

I fell back asleep,
And dreamed about the snow,
How soft it is, how soft it blows.

Lauren Oldaker (13)
Heathfield Foundation High School

DECISION

When I look into the mirror what do I see?
My blonde hair, my lips, my nose, my eyes,
My face?
No I see shame -
A failure to my parents,
A disgrace to my family,
Why I hear you ask?
What could a girl of thirteen, barely part of society
have done to be this?
It's simple.
I made *one* bad decision which changed my life.
I've said I'm sorry,
I've opened my heart to try and justify my decision,
But they ask why?
Why would I do this?
I reply with meaningless and feeble excuses,
Which they don't understand.
I felt lonely, confused, lost,
If I could have only known the cost.

Rebecca Parker-Compton (13)
Heathfield Foundation High School

AUTUMN

Leaves on the ground,
They're all around.
You can't see the floor,
You can't get through the door.

As the children start to scream,
The spooks come up for Hallowe'en.
They ask for money or a sweet,
Then run the adults up the street.

Children watch without a sound,
As the fireworks leave the ground.
Sparklers are so very bright,
Safe for children on Bonfire Night.

Adam Polito (13)
Heathfield Foundation High School

HALLOWE'EN

H orrid witches come out to play,
A ll at once you hear them say,
L aughing and cackling in the night,
L ittle children get a fright,
O nly ghouls and ghosts walk the streets alone,
W ailing and squealing do they ever moan,
E ach in a torment all of their own,
E very little ghost is all bone and skin,
N ever to be seen again.

Daniel Aston (13)
Heathfield Foundation High School

HALLOWE'EN

It's Hallowe'en today,
The children are excited,
When we get back from school,
We can go 'trick or treating'.

I am wearing my witch's outfit,
My brother is wearing his vampire outfit,
Our tricks can be to squirt vampire blood,
Our treats will be so great we will turn out fat.

I will scare the people with my glowing pumpkin
And I will scare them with my outfit,
We will eat lots of toffee apples
And be fat at the end of Hallowe'en.

Hayley Cronin (13)
Heathfield Foundation High School

THE MELON

It is as yellow as the morning sun,
It hits my taste buds like a gun.
It's as smooth as a baby's bum,
I prefer it to chewing gum.

It's as big as a giant's eye,
It lightens me up like the big blue sky.
It's the shape of a rugby ball,
I wish they'd serve it in the dinner hall.

The melon is beautiful
In many different ways.
I wish I could eat one
Every single day.

Kyle Lal (13)
Heathfield Foundation High School

CHRISTMAS DAY

Not a murmur in the house
As I creep downstairs
To see what presents await me
As my family starts to come downstairs
One by one.

We sit there excited, opening our presents
Which are under the Christmas tree
With smiles on our faces,
I looked out of the window
The ground is like cotton wool.

I could smell the turkey cooking in the oven,
With little sausages lying next to it,
It smelt gorgeous.
While all the family gather in the living room
Dinner is ready to be served, oh what a feast.

Out comes the champagne bottles,
Pop it goes as the cork goes flying across the room.
As the night gets later it starts to snow harder,
But we're all in the warmth.
The day has come to an end and it is time to go to bed.

Jenna Saunders (13)
Heathfield Foundation High School

HALLOWE'EN

The blackness of the night scares everyone around,
All you hear is the running of feet on the ground.
Then a knock at your door and you jump from your seat
And there's a child dressed up saying *'Trick or Treat.'*

Then you'll carefully choose which one you will have,
Be generous, give money or put your hand in that bag.
And as you decide to give is the best,
You'll sigh with relief you got rid of the pest.

Jodie Ashman (13)
Heathfield Foundation High School

HALLOWE'EN

It's nearly Hallowe'en,
6 years old to a teen.
If you're bright
and you like a fright,
then come along on Hallowe'en.

It's time to trick or treat.
Good fun and lots to eat.
Ghosts who moan
and you're on your own,
I can't wait to get my treats.

When Hallowe'en is here
everyone feels a bit of fear.
If you're with a group of friends,
the fun will never end.
There was a lot of tears.

Now Hallowe'en has gone,
All the tears and fear, there is none.
There's still some candy
and a mask, which is handy,
when Hallowe'en comes round again.

Kerry Jordan (13)
Heathfield Foundation High School

CHRISTMAS DAY

The coldness of early Christmas morning filled us with glee
And the excitement of tearing Christmas paper apart.
We lay in bed thinking about the good that was going to happen today.

My family and I ran down the stairs
And lots of presents were under the tree decorated with bright lights.

Eagerly we tear at the paper, surprises await us,
Tension then smiles and laughter, the present was just what I wanted.

Nice smells escaping from the kitchen,
A table laden with festive morsels.
Crackers ready to pull
And at last the great feast arrives.

The turkey cut and pudding eaten,
Tummies full and ready to explode.
A sleep is what we need,
So goodnight everybody,
Another Christmas Day is over again.

Emma Bridgewood (13)
Heathfield Foundation High School

A POEM ABOUT SEASONS

Snowflakes sitting on the window sills,
Children outside getting chills.
Soft snow like glitter sparkles in the sun,
The children outside still having fun.

Autumn leaves float to the ground,
They go round, and round as they come down.
Soft oranges and reds,
As we snuggle up in our beds.

Summer sun, soft, gentle breeze,
Rustling leaves make sound from the trees.
Birds whistling in the skies,
With really colourful butterflies.

Green grass in the meadows,
With very happy fellows.
Newborn lambs, chickens too,
I think spring is great, do you?

Naomi Amphlett (13)
Heathfield Foundation High School

THE 31ST OF OCTOBER

Pumpkins glowing in the windows,
Dusk travels along the street,
Trick or treaters knock on the door,
And ring the bell, scary mask and all.

The sun goes down, the night draws in,
A gauntlet of darkening wood,
The moon hides behind the clouds,
And the lights keep on flickering, I wonder why?

People are frightened of ghosts
And witches.
The people start to go to bed,
The 31st of October is near enough dead.

Alex Giles (13)
Heathfield Foundation High School

SPRING HAS BEGUN

I have heard a mother bird
Singing in the rain -
Telling all her little ones
Spring has come again.

I have seen a wave of green
Down a lovely lane -
Making all the hedges glad
Spring has come again.

I have found a patch of ground
Golden in the sun;
Crocuses are calling out
Spring has just begun!

Joanne Coley (13)
Heathfield Foundation High School

HALLOWE'EN

H   allowe'en is a night to remember,
A   ll is dark and quiet,
L   aughter heard from miles around,
L   ike people in a riot,
O   ranges, chocolates, sweets and more,
W   arlocks and ghosts, witches and wizards,
E   very child with a collecting bowl,
E   ventually fills the pot,
N   ow eat, what a lot they've got!

Jade Sharman (13)
Heathfield Foundation High School

THE UNNOTICED BOY

Weather defines me
Rained down as every day
I sit in a dull corner,
I'll have a say that sunny day.

But
I did not speak a word,
My voice makes me angry
As I sit in my dull corner,
People pull faces at me.

I dare not breathe,
I dare not whisper,
I sit all alone,
I'm getting bitter.

But
I grow through my path,
Soon I will die.
I'm getting older,
I wish I could fly.

Suddenly
I'm getting much stronger,
I'm now past that weakness,
I've reached success,
I've climbed my way up the steepness.

Now it's sunny
When I wake up every day.
I hear my voice clearly,
I've now had my say that sunny day.

Amit Puri (13)
Heathfield Foundation High School

BONFIRE NIGHT

B urning flames shine up bright,
O range fireworks in the night,
N aughty children throw logs in the fire,
F ire crackles but does not expire.
I see the colours,
R ed, white and others
E ntering into the dark, black night.

N ear to the fire,
I ntense is the heat,
G rease-covered hot dogs, providing something to eat,
H ere we are, having fun,
T he night is still young.

Razwana Ali (13)
Heathfield Foundation High School

HALLOWE'EN

H allowe'en is the one night of the year when the dead can arise
A nd witches and goblins fly about in the skies.
L ooking at the sky you can see the Devil's face
L aughing and chortling all over the place.
O ver the hills and far away.
W icked old women cast spells all day.
E ven at night you can hear the wolves howl,
E ventually you will hear them all sigh.
N ever in the rest of the year will you see the witches fly.

Louise Siviter (13)
Heathfield Foundation High School

CHRISTMAS AT OUR HOUSE

Christmas is a time for fun,
Cards and gifts for everyone.
Wrapping paper being torn
And all for a baby being born.
We eat lots of turkey,
Until we're not perky.
Watching the telly,
Teasing our Shelly.
Drinking our souls away
We awake in the morning
Feeling sick and yawning
And that is our Christmas Day.

James Keefe (13)
Heathfield Foundation High School

BONFIRE NIGHT

B angs and flashes of bright colours
O range flashing lights a-blare
N o one hates the glamour and flare
F ires in the night sky
I love to see the fireworks fly
R ipping through the autumn air
E ven when it's cold out there

N eon lights from the fair
I ndigo, violet, they're all there
G etting into the midnight flare
H aving loads of fun at the fair
T onight's the night, it will all be there.

Amy Finch (13)
Heathfield Foundation High School

THE WITCH

There was a witch with a wart on her nose
And on her feet, mouldy green toes.
On her head she wore a pointy black hat
Her stomach was big round and fat.

On the night of Hallowe'en
She's always to be seen.
On her broomstick flying high
High up in the dark black sky.

If you saw her on this dark black night
You would surely have a fright.
So beware on the night of Hallowe'en
The big fat witch will always be seen!

Martin Giles (13)
Heathfield Foundation High School

HALLOWE'EN

H aunting ghosts through the night on the 31st October
A t every minute of the night, knocking and howling.
L onely souls wander the streets.
L ater on children wander trick or treating
O nly ghouls and ghosts come out at night.
W itches flying on broomsticks with cats, dark as night
E vil witches make stew in the cauldron
E vil devils haunt the towns
N early time for bed but that's the end of Hallowe'en.

Charlotte Melvin (13)
Heathfield Foundation High School

CHRISTMAS

C hristmas night is also bright
H ave a laugh and cry all night
R ipping open presents of joy
I nside is a gift for a boy
S anta Claus is coming to town
T rees decorated red and brown
M en and women dancing around
A lthough there is a happy, joyful sound.
S nogging under the mistletoe.

Sam Jones (13)
Heathfield Foundation High School

THE MILLENNIUM

The millennium's coming,
It's nearly here.
Only eight more hours,
Until the end of the year.

Balloons are flying,
Parties everywhere.
I can't wait,
Until the millennium's here.

We arrive at the party,
It's going to be great.
The millennium's nearly here,
I just can't wait.

The clock strikes twelve,
Everyone cheers.
Finally, at last,
The millennium's here.

Laura Leanne Haynes (12)
Menzies High School

LESSONS

Science is boring
And so is French
And English
And maths
And geography
And music
And assembly
And RE.

Art is good
And technology
And so is PE.

Kevin Antill (13)
Millfield School

SCHOOL LESSONS

I have art on a Friday.
I like science, it is good.
I like French, French is fun.
I like PE, I like gymnastics.
I like assembly.
I like being pupil of the week.
I like geography.
I like music
I like going home.
When I go home I listen to my music.

Anne Layland (13)
Millfield School

SCHOOL FRIENDS

Friends are good
Friends can help
Friends can be there for you.

Some friends are boys
Some friends are girls
Some friends are funny.

Friends can be sad
Friends can be nasty
Friends can be alright.

Some friends I like
Some friends I don't like
But friends are good to have.

Emma Meachin (13)
Millfield School

FRIENDS AT SCHOOL

Friends can play football.
Friends can help.
Friends are good.
Friends are funny.
Friends can play basketball.
Friends can be there for you.
Friends are nasty
Friends are alright
Friends are good to have.

Richard May (13)
Millfield School

WHAT'S GOOD AT SCHOOL

PE is good at school
It's good when we play basketball
It's good when we win.

Art is good at school
It's good when we print
It's good when we paint.

Playtime is good at school
We don't have to do any work
We can talk when we want to.

Home time is good at school
When I get home I go out
I love home time.

Sarah Roy (13)
Millfield School

SCHOOL LESSONS

French is boring.
Science is OK.
English is not good.
RE is boring.

Geography is good.
PE is brilliant.
Maths are OK.
Technology is wicked.

David Hall (13)
Millfield School

SCHOOL POEM

I don't want to be naughty.
I want to be good
so that I can go
on a trip.

I want friends.
Friends want me.
Friends want me to go too
Go kids go with them.

I like football.
Football makes
me happy.
I am happy
when I score a *goal!*

Kieron Howen (13)
Millfield School

TEACHERS

Some teachers are boring
Some teachers are good
Some teachers are funny
Some are like Miss Wood.

French and maths are boring
Science and art are good
Music and geography are funny
But I like going to Miss Wood.

Gareth Jones (13)
Millfield School

MY PONY

My pony's my friend,
She means everything to me,
Her name is Misty!
She can be very nifty.

With coat of grey,
I love to hear her neigh,
While dashing round the paddock,
Causing such havoc.

With her bright, shining coat,
Long mane of hair,
Eyes bright, like the morning star,
Her gallop, as fleet as the wind,
She's all a pet should be.

Feeding her in the morning,
Grooming her down,
I'd much rather be with her,
Than go shopping in town.

My Misty is a mystery, that is a fact,
Her funny little moods,
Like standing on my foot,
Or butting me in the back.

You can keep your dogs,
Keep your cats,
Give me my Misty every time,
I'm so glad she's all mine,
Well, most of the time.

Emma Shinton (12)
Summerhill School

OUR HOLIDAY DREAM

We all go on holiday,
Every summer we do,
We all pack our things,
And put them in the boot.

We all drive across the motorway,
To the airport we go,
Then we catch the plane,
Our holiday dream's coming true.

It maybe to
America, France or Spain
But at least we go on holiday
Now and again.

As we get out of the plane,
It's a lovely, hot, fresh breeze,
When we take the first step
It seems like a dream.

Once we have collected our stuff,
We go to the hotel,
Now we have got our room
And take a look around.

Now we have got our holiday spirit
We go for a swim,
Maybe to the beach,
Or an explore around the village.

We are on our way back home,
On the aeroplane again,
We're sorry that it's ended,
The end of our holiday dream.

Jessica Swinscoe (12)
Summerhill School

THE OLDEN DAYS

The world around us as we see
Isn't how it used to be.
Children weren't allowed to play
They had to work real hard all day.
Sweeping, cleaning, washing too,
That's what the children had to do.
Even if a child fell ill,
They would have to pay for the medical bill.
The kings and queens got it easy,
That makes me mad, that makes me queasy.
Most of the children couldn't do
Different things, like me and you.
Skating, football, netball too,
That's what the children wished they could do.
My mam and dad once said to me,
'The world isn't how it used to be.'

Charlotte Collins (12)
Summerhill School

POD RACING!

They line up on the starting line,
They're about to start the race.
When the lights give the sign,
They'll zoom off at fast pace.

They start the race at the speed of light,
As they go through the caves.
To come first they have to fight,
Their own lives they try to save.

As their engines roar,
The crowds cheer.
They get faster more and more,
The racers are struck with fear.

The finish line is in sight,
A final thrust takes the lead.
They accelerate with all their might,
To finish at lightning speed.

Simon McDermott (11)
Summerhill School

OUR TV

There it sits, a blank screen,
Just waiting,
Waiting for anyone to put a programme on it,
Any event to show anyone willing to look,
When I stare at the blank screen,
It just sits there, a plain and empty world,
With nowhere to go,
All alone with no one to talk to,
With no one to care.
It sits alone all day, every day
In its own little world.
It is clever when we think about it,
It's a big box which sits all day storing information
Of everyone's favourite show,
Of everyone's favourite channel.
In fact, when I really think about it,
I don't know what I would do without my TV.

Hannah Davis (12)
Summerhill School

BROTHERS

I hate brothers when they scream and bawl
Especially when you've done nothing at all.

My brother gets away with murder and I get all the blame
I think he's nasty and a massive pain.

I hate brothers, they're nasty and mean
He shouts at me and makes me scream, scream, scream.

As you can imagine, I'm never a pain
My brother's the one who's always to blame.

I hate brothers when they scream and bawl
Especially when you've done nothing at all.

Nichola Walker (12)
Summerhill School

MOTOCROSS

Motocross is about racing on motorbikes around a dirty track
People who do motocross are well experienced
When you start you cannot turn back
If you get close you're bound for a smack
Red light, red light, green, go
People cheering as you go
You see the finish line, one more turn to go
Petrol out, not enough time to wait
Watch out you're in for a wait
You come last sitting in disgust
But don't worry you're back on track.

Chris Hewitt (11)
Summerhill School

SLEEPOVER

Sarah came round on Friday night,
We started off with a pillow fight.
Sarah came down to see my mice,
She held them and thought they were very nice.
We saw my dog and then my cat,
We did Zorba's dance and looked very fat!
We went upstairs to watch some telly,
Molly the dog jumped on my belly.
We laughed until we could not stop -
I thought my belly was going to pop!
We lazed about and had a chat,
Mum shouted 'Do you have to be noisy like that?'
We had a pizza - mushroom and ham,
(I would have preferred a sandwich with jam)
We ate and ate until we were full,
Not even once did we think about school!
We stayed awake till 3 o'clock,
If Mum had known, she'd have a shock.
I thought really Mum did know
But I thought she wasn't letting it show.
Because we were as quiet as mice,
My dad thought it was very nice.
I hope a sleepover happens again
Because Sarah is really a very good friend!

Lucy Hill (11)
Summerhill School

THE MAN WHO LIKED JELLO

There once was an old man,
Who lived in a caravan.
He lived with his cat,
Who quite often sat,
In a very old cushion chair.

This man was a jolly good fellow,
He liked to eat lots of jello,
Which he found in a cave,
Which gave him a crave,
To return for more every day.

Unknown to the man in the cave,
Waited a dragon to make him a slave,
Who planted the jello,
To bring forth the fellow,
To turn him into a slave.

All went well until one day,
Then to the dragon the man fell prey,
So the man called for a slay of the dragon,
So another man came riding a wagon,
Who happened to be a dragon slayer.

So out burst a fight,
Through the sword and the light,
Then out came the man,
Who just made a fan,
Came out waiting for his payment.

I have no way to pay you,
Now I don't believe that is true,
You look like a nice fellow
Who does not eat jello,
So hand all that over to me.

So then the fellow,
Handed over the jello,
He then thanked him for doing the slay
And sent the good man on his way
And lived happily ever after.

Nathan Robinson (12)
Summerhill School

COLD, COLD WORLD

One half of the world lives in warm houses,
With double glazing and central heating,
Watching TV and laughing at jokes,
they have no worries.

The other half lives in small mud huts,
With one room and no door,
Wondering if they will survive tomorrow,
Every day is a constant struggle.

One half of the world eats a huge Sunday dinner,
The other half of the world has no food to eat
and wonders 'Will there ever?'
One half of the world gives their children to a nanny
The other half finds their baby is dead
and is grateful it's not their cow instead.
While one half lives,
The other dies.
I bet you're glad you're red
and not blue instead.

Sean Ennis (12)
Summerhill School

SKATING

At night I go skating in the park,
I stay out until it gets dark
My friends come out to play with me,
But later on they go in for tea.

When we go out we skate round and round,
Then we go to the shop to spend our pound.
At 6:50pm I leave my mates
To get home for 7:00pm hoping not to be late.

The next day at school I go to form time,
In English I have to make up a rhyme.
I ask my friends if they're coming out tonight,
They say they're going out, but later they might.

My mom said I've got pizza for tea,
Because you have got to share it with me.
I asked my mom what time to come in?
'Come in at 7:00pm or your tea's in the bin.

I put my skates on and skated around,
Then I realised there was no one to be found.
I went home and went on the phone,
The phone kept ringing, there was nobody home.

I want to go out and have some fun,
It's cold later on because there's no sun.
I wonder where everyone's gone,
There's no one out, no fun, no one.

Later on my friends came out to play,
They stayed out for the rest of the day.
Sam, can I borrow . . .
Oh, it's 6:60, I'll ask you tomorrow!

When I got home I didn't think I was late,
But I heard the clock ting as I opened the gate!

Rebecca Wood (11)
Summerhill School

FRIENDS

Friends.
What are friends?
Someone to share the good times with,
Someone to share the bad times with.
Someone with a friendly shoulder,
Always there when you need them.

Friends are the people who cheer you up,
Friends are there when you need a hug.
Sometimes they get mad
And you'll fall out,
But you'll always make up,
Without a doubt.
When I get lonely, they're just at the end of the phone
And they'll listen to me moan.
When I'm feeling sad and blue,
I can always count on them to make me smile.
My friends,
They'll always be there for me.

Leanne Rathore (11)
Summerhill School

THE DETENTION

I was sitting down,
Thinking of a noun,
In my after-school detention
When a spider caught my attention.
I crushed it with my pen,
When Mrs Ken,
An animal lover,
Saw my little endeavour.
I lied
And said 'It just died!'
And Mrs Ken wasn't keen
On my little scheme.
And that got me into more trouble
And my detention became a double.
So let that be a lesson to all
That think detentions are cool.

Andrew Thornton (11)
Summerhill School

LOVE

Love is what,
Love is who,
Love is what blossoms between me and you,
It might be good,
It might be bad,
But love will drive you flippin' mad.

At first it will just be a fling,
Then a thing,
Then before you know it, you're fully wed,
With a veil on your head.
So at the end of the day,
You will feel quite gay,
And that is all I'm going to say.

Jonathan Tomlinson (13)
Summerhill School

F1 'GRAND PRIX'

The lights of the 'Grand Prix' go:
Red, red, red, red, red.
The cars are revving
Rev, rev, rev, the lights are out
the commentator says 'Go, go, go'
They are going round the first corner at top speed
Brmm, brmm, brmm
Someone's lost control
Oh no, there's a pile up
Crash, crash
What a mess. The commentator screams
Red flag out
Stop race! Stop race!
The race is stopped, someone's injured
The crowd are silent - their man's injured
The marshal's thumb raises
Their man is all right
The race has been abandoned
Too many cars out
Too much mess!

Nathan Jones (11)
Summerhill School

THE THUNDERSTORM

The sky went cloudy and black,
The birds went quiet and
Suddenly, *crack!*
Lightning flashed and
The rain started falling,
Babies, bawling
Water fell and roads were wet,
Along time ago the sun had set,
Thunder clapped and
car doors locked,
the gutter's broke,
Water choked
Thoughts of sea
came down on my,
The rain beat down on a distant shore,
My mind came back with a knock on the door,
Soaked cat lying on the floor,
I felt sorry for the poor little mite,
Shivering and cold in all its fright,
An outbreak of thunder rose again,
1-2 minutes away, in-between rain,
Then quiet once again!

Robert Sansom (11)
Summerhill School

THE LAGOON

For as long as I can remember,
The village was still,
Until a great storm swept over the hill,
What appeared after was a shock.

A surfboard right through a tree,
And Miss Tilly no longer in the sea!
Now we have ninety seconds between a tidal wave.

I must shelter,
I mustn't get wet.
But you remember the story,
And watch out for that tidal wave!

Paul Harwood (11)
Summerhill School

SPORT

I like football
I like playing it
I like scoring
I like getting sent off.

I like cricket
I like playing it
I like scoring runs
I like getting people out.

I like tennis
I like playing it
I like scoring points
I like knocking people out.

I like boxing
I like playing it
I like winning rounds
I like hurting people.

I like rugby
I like playing it
I like winning games
I like getting tries.

Stephen Hawkins (11)
Summerhill School

THE LITTLE BROWN DOG

Slowly a dog walks along,
Waiting for the early bird's song,
With his weak little paws,
And his very long, sharp claws.

With his little tiny heart,
All he wants is to be a part
When people are in fear
He cried out a little tear.

When he woke up at morning rise
He did wake up with a big surprise.
There was an open door
And children letting him onto their floor.

Amy Moran (11)
Summerhill School

THE FOX

All is quiet in the forest one day
The fox comes out of his hole to play
When all of a sudden he hears a sound
The fox darts back to his hole in the ground.

The sound he heard was an old bloodhound
So the fox goes deeper into the ground
All of a sudden he hears some hooves
The sound gets less and less all around
So the fox comes out of his hole to play
For another day.

James Donald (11)
Summerhill School

MY HORSE MARTY

My pony is my friend,
his name is Marty,
he means everything to me,
his coat is a palomino kind.

With his bright shiny coat
and his long shiny mane,
his hoofs so nice and clean,
he is definitely one of a kind.

I love going to see him,
although he is rather naughty,
I still love him,
I love feeding him in the morning,
when the sun is just dawning.

Charlotte Marks (12)
Summerhill School

BYE BYE

Bye bye, see you soon,
Miss you already, come home soon,
I miss your laughter, your joy, your smile.

I can remember your face through a day in the fields,
Your hair blowing so slightly in the wind,
Your bright blue eyes glittering in the sun.

Bye bye sis, luv you so, be safe up there,
Come home soon, I miss you so,
Good luck up there, that big, strong place,
Get a good job, buy me a pressie,
Come home soon, luv you so.

Sarah Day (12)
Summerhill School

CHOCOLATE!

Chocolate is great, when you have a mate,
To eat with your mate at a gate,
Going to the park with your mate,
Waking up thinking you're late.

Waking up thinking you're late,
Dreaming about chocolate,
Going to school, eating it with your mate
And doing the work and writing the date

And going to lessons trying to be late,
You're trying to eat some chocolate,
Going to lessons and being late,
Getting told off by your mate.

Going home with your mate,
Going to the shops to buy chocolate,
Going home, being late,
Mom is wondering why you are late.

Going to the park,
Playing with your mate on the park,
Going home thinking I'm not awake,
Mom is asking why you're not awake!

Hannah Yates (11)
Summerhill School

MIDSUMMER NIGHT'S DANCE

She slowly wrapped her ribbons high,
Criss-cross, over and under.
The satin fabric so soft she tied,
So red, glittery and tender.

She stood up like a picture,
About to wish a star.
Her hair whistled through the sky,
Like a wanderer from a fair.

She lifted her arms over her head,
Pointed her toe and rose above.
Her strong figure glistened in the moonlight,
But the footsteps so soft like a dove.

Twirling, twisting on the tip of her toe,
Stretching and lifting her arms.
Skipping and galloping, legs up high
And twirled her palm.

As the sun rose,
The dance died
But tomorrow you see
The dance will arise.

Stevie Beddoe (12)
Summerhill School

DANCING

Dancing,
Starting fast
Ending slow
Changing positions from high to low.
On your toes, on your feet
So much to do
And so much to see.
Whether it's ballet or whether it's tap
You always know you're in for a laugh
Jumping high to the sky
Landing low on your toe
Different music,
Different sounds
Some ballerinas look like clowns
At the end, take a bow
Naughty behaviour we *do not* allow.

Charlotte Rolinson (11)
Summerhill School

SCORPION IN STOMACH

Crawling through my body a dirty brown scorpion,
Stinging my insides, my head, my feet, my thighs.
Coldness builds inside me making me ferment,
A slithering snake decides to join the pain,
Hissing softly, smoothly in my head,
Feeling I am drinking a witch's potion,
Bubbling in my body like a volcano
That melts the coldness when it erupts.

Sara Khan (12)
Swanshurst School

SCHOOL DINNERS

Every day, every day, school dinners every day
Every day it's the same old way
Walk in, wait and wait
Grab plate, grab food
Same old thing, same old way
Pay for it, go sit down
Eat it up, go outside
Stand in the cold, freeze to death
Yet if we didn't have school dinners
We'd be eating out in the cold
Nowhere to sit, nowhere to eat
But inside it's nice and warm
Warm food, warm canteen
School dinners - plenty to eat!

Sobiah Sheereen (12)
Swanshurst School

RUBBISH DUMP

A baby had a tantrum
She threw her toys all around
Old washing machines and broken trees
Scattered on the ground
A giant's toys are on the ground
Some are really new
A tumble dryer without knobs
A bike with no wheels
An old stuffed Winnie the Pooh
A giant's toys are all around
You can barely see the floor
Will anyone ever pick them up?
This place is *such a dump.*

Sophie Williams (12)
Swanshurst School

To Wear Or Not To Wear

We want to wear the latest fashion
But school uniform is in our way
We pay for a non uniform day
Fashion is our greatest passion
Fashion all across the English nation
Children wanting their way every day
Complaining from June to May
Fashion is the world's greatest creation
But maybe uniform is useful
It could stop us from getting teased
By others who are scary and tall
Just because of clothes that are unfashionable
Maybe the pressure is eased
Maybe uniform isn't bad at all.

Emily Finnimore (12)
Swanshurst School

Seaside

How many times have I ever wondered
What lies beneath the waves?
How many times have I ever wondered
What is inside those caves?

Is it a starfish, red and blue,
Or a chest of treasure, bright?
Is it a fish with glowing hue,
Or just darkness, black as night?

Is it a skeleton with whitish bones,
Or an anemone, red as blood?
Is it a snail with a bright top shell,
Or just thick and sandy mud?

Is it dark green bubbly seaweed
Whose fronds flow with the tide,
Or is it a bristle worm, long and slender,
That moves from side to side?

Jessica Harrison (12)
Swanshurst School

MOTORWAY MANIA!

(An Italian sonnet about the building of even more motorways)

Getting from A to B would be quicker,
You won't be late so it won't spoil your plans,
You won't worry about getting in jams,
You won't get stressed or get even sicker.
Public transport makes you mad, so you bicker,
In buses you're so hot, that you need fans,
You need peace and space; instead you're cramped,
In cars on motorways, you feel fitter.
But what about the animals, we're destroying their homes,
They're being killed a thousand every second,
It's not green now, it looks so much worse,
Now where do the little animals roam?
They'll be scared of the engines that'll beckon,
Just for the benefit of all of us.

Jane Miles (12)
Swanshurst School

THE HUNTSMEN

The huntsmen in red like a bit of sport
They think foxing is really good fun
They kill the chickens, but never get caught
They're off like a shot if they hear a gun
The huntsmen will kill foxes of all sorts
When the foxes are killed, their work is done
The dead foxes they've killed weigh a tonne
Guns kill the foxes which the men import
But they kill foxes who don't need to die
The huntsmen don't realise that it's cruel
If foxes could speak, then see how they'd moan
If foxes die out, you will know why
I think there should be a foxing rule
That all foxes should be left well alone.

Rebecca Underdown (13)
Swanshurst School

WILL I BE A MURDERER?

Why murder something so cute and so small,
When it's so helpless and very sweet,
Guilty! After stopping its small heartbeat,
You should protect them don't let them fall,
Invest in adoption it is not cruel,
You are not alone others feel the heat,
Don't be scared, don't run away, please don't flee,
But then again did you not mean it,
You don't want a child at 14, do you?
Do you know why you bothered with men?
The baby might be ill and suffer fits,
If you have the baby you both might die,
You should wait a few years and have it then.

Helen Ginnis (12)
Swanshurst School

THE BEAR'S NOT THE FOOL

Bear bating is very entertaining,
It is fun to watch, you get a big thrill,
Especially when you see the blood spill.
You don't hear anybody complaining
Although the bears get a great big caning.
It is fun to watch the bears kill
But it is completely against the bears' will.
No free time, as it's perform then training
Making them dance is not natural
And they do not want rings through their noses.
Whipping the bears hurts and it's cruel
But to the audience it's satisfactual.
You're just making them do silly poses
You may think they're stupid but you're the fool.

Jenny Boilestad (12)
Swanshurst School

ALL THAT'S SMALL

All that's small in the world,
They are bent, straight, even curled.
Green and black, maybe red,
Some are snuggled up in bed.
Reeds and leaves are best places,
Can't see their smiley faces.
Shadows hide the smallest creatures,
Even ones with special features.
Hidden in the leaves of green,
Small creatures can't be seen.
Mice, slugs, earwigs galore,
Rats, hedgehogs, snails and more.

Emma Willis (12)
Swanshurst School

SILENT SNOW WORLD

The sparkling, silent land,
A new world under a soft blanket of pretty snow,
Small green firs with magical white,
There is no need to turn on a light,
In the silent snow world.

A young sweet bird wakes from sleep,
She puts out her head and out comes a tweet,
The silent snow world is not so silent,
The world is now beginning to waken.

A small child lets out a whimper,
She will soon be dressed to face the cold winter.
She eats a warm breakfast,
It is her favourite,
Sugared porridge.

A silent snow world it is no longer,
It is a child's fancy and wonder.
Small little footsteps breaking the snow,
My spirits sink so, so low,
It is a silent world no longer.

Jainey Mun (12)
Swanshurst School

ANIMALS DON'T COME FOR FREE

Animals are much cheaper than mankind
They don't really matter very much
There's plenty more out of the hutch
Animals don't have feelings they won't mind
They're so dumb and they're easy to find
Animal lives don't add up to much
Their lives and their minds don't keep in touch.
They rely on us, we're their crutch.
But maybe animals do matter and care
Animals would rather be free to play
They're taken for granted, misunderstood
And maybe somehow I was being unfair
We must care if we want them to stay
We must be humane if we want them to stay.

Megan Owen (13)
Swanshurst School

NIGHTMARES

N ightmares are gruesome, dreadful, frightful dreams,
I magination runs wild, terrifying you.
G ruesome beasts and monsters suddenly appear,
H aunted houses, gigantic spiders, blood and guts.
T hey are things that appear in nightmares,
M urderers wiping out the human race,
A ll around me is blood and all the things I hate,
R unning for my life trying to escape.
E verywhere the eye can see is evil,
S creaming loudly, but no one hears.

Kyle Newton (12)
Windsor High School

WILL THEY EVER UNDERSTAND?

What they do is so boring,
Diagnosing bad things,
Who gets fun out of that?
When they get home they moan about stress,
But they don't see what the patients see,

When we don't understand,
They smile smugly,
Trying to understand just makes it harder,
They don't really try to explain in English
Just in their language.

Just ask this when you're angry
Will they ever hear bad news?
No,
Have they ever been through it?
No,
So will they ever understand?
No.

If you know who *they* are,
You've been through it too,
For the rest of you it's
Doctors!

Lisa Bloomer (13)
Windsor High School

TRICK OR TREAT

The wind whispers through the trees,
The witching hour grows near,
The mist settles on the ground,
My body fills with fear.

Lightning flashes, thunder clashes,
Pumpkins gleam and children scream,
Why? Because it's Hallowe'en,
To most it's just a bit of fun,
But it's enough to make me run!

Claire Weale (12)
Windsor High School

HELP ME!

'Help me! Please,
I've lost my keys,
Oh! Help me come on
Before I'm told off by Mr Gleeze,
So won't you help me find my keys?'
He said: 'I don't have time,
I have to go at nine,
Oh I'm so sorry brother of mine.'

'Help me! Please,
Could they be by the cheese,
I need to find them now,
He is very strict that Mr Gleeze,
So won't you help me find my keys?'
He said: 'I'm sorry but I'm late,
I must get to the school gate,
I am sorry but you will have to wait.'

'Help me! Please,
I need your advice . . .
Will £10 suffice?'
He said: 'Well hey what are brothers for,
Tell you what if I find them quick how about £5 more?'

Thomas Henderson (13)
Windsor High School

THE BUFFALO HUNT

The grass stretched as far as I could see,
The buffaloes did not seem frightened of me,
They were tall and strong and bursting with power,
But to me they looked like they could not hurt a flower,
I burst out of the grass with all my might,
Shooting arrows at the nearest thing in sight.
The herd moved quickly,
But I stayed close by,
I charged at them and cried my warrior cry,
Most of the herd went away,
But this one big bull decided to stay.
It advanced and began to paw the ground
I fired my arrows, they flew without sound.
With my last arrow in my bow,
I covered my eyes and thought 'Oh no'
When I opened my eyes I was clutching my head
But when I looked up the big bull was dead.

David James Sutton (11)
Windsor High School

HEDGEHOG

Something's twitching in the leaves,
leaving paws in the mud, chewing away at the bugs.
In gardens and in fields the hedgehog moves,
trying to find a nice home.
Slowly and carefully across the road,
at last the hedgehog finds a home,
where he is free to roam and far from danger.

Matthew Peniket (13)
Windsor High School

AND IT HAPPENED AGAIN!

Why do tragedies happen?
I don't know,
Do you?
The carriages are everywhere,
Crumpled up like concertinas,
The people inside them won't come out!
Survivors and friends stand around like the dead.
How could it happen . . . again?
Everyone searches for someone to blame,
The driver?
The government?
Not themselves!
They promised it wouldn't happen again
But it did
And it's worse!
We all ask,
Can we stop it happening again
And again
And again?

Stephanie Hardy (13)
Windsor High School

THE TELESCOPE

Gazing into the darkness
Seeing twinkling stars
Like glitter on black velvet
If you're lucky you will see a shooting star
There is not one word that can describe it all.

Stuart Brown (13)
Windsor High School

THE SUNSHINE

People think the sun has a smiley waking face,
But it doesn't,
It has a special place,
In the sky
And in our hearts.
As I look into your eyes the sun shines back at me
And the world is a better place.
Suddenly I see things in a different way,
War is no longer upon us,
All I see is you
And as you brush your hair back with your hand,
My heart now does understand,
That you and me,
Were meant to be,
Together forever,
Always.
Now we've grown old through the thick and the thin,
Our time is near gone,
But yet not far away,
I can still remember what you did say,
Lou' my dear love,
Will you marry me?

Sarah Bowen (13)
Windsor High School

I HAVE A DREAM!

'I have a dream.'
So said by Martin Luther King,
When he won the Nobel Prize.
What was his dream I wonder?
To make friends with the white,
To walk in peace and harmony
Along the streets of America.

He was assassinated in '68
Before his dream came true,
His followers made it come true
For the good of all mankind
I wonder how he felt
As he turned in his grave.

Kerri Bissell (13)
Windsor High School

TIME

Time they say is like a straight corridor
No going back, a one-way system
Or perhaps it's just hard to navigate
You need a map
Or a bike to slip through the traffic of the
crowded one-way system that is our lives.

Maybe it's a motorway, high speed, no stopping
Until the fuel runs out or you have an accident
But on this motorway you must be careful not to
speed
Because when you crash there is always a
pile-up
You can never repair the dents in the body work
Or the scratches on the paint work

Some people's cars go round tiny ring-roads
Faster and faster and faster getting nowhere
Until they take a detour and start to enjoy
life for once
Not speeding
Taking in the scenery and relaxing
Like we all should in today's hectic world.

Peter Wagstaff (12)
Windsor High School

MY PHOBIA OF VENTRILOQUISTS' DUMMIES

Awake,
Can't sleep,
Coming,
Coming closer,
Coming for me,
Closer,
Closer!

Very scared,
Terribly frightened,
Amazingly horrified,
Incredibly petrified,
Of dummies.

Chilling, painted eyes,
Clunking, wooden feet,
Floppy, lifeless arms,
Cruel, staring faces,
Dummies!

Naomi Reed (12)
Windsor High School

GHOSTS AND GHOULS

Ghosts and ghouls and apparitions come out at night
to haunt and scare.
The repugnant faces, the daunting experiences,
the frightening feeling that someone's watching you!
Ghosts and ghouls are everywhere,
be careful ghouls and creeps might be after you.
They creep around the graveyard as quiet as mice,
when they join together a big scream and . . .

Benjamin Davies (12)
Windsor High School

SPIDERS!

I see the spider web in the corner
The web glistening from the sun
There and then the spider came crawling down the web
Watching its every move, scared to move from my chair
Praying it will fall so I can stamp on it.

Its hairy legs and its eyes just stare
All thoughts run through my head
Oh my God! It's climbing down the wall
Mum, Mum please come help
The spider's climbing down the wall.

No one answered. I'm all alone with the hairy spider
It's glistening in the sunlight
It's on the floor coming my way
Oh please spider, just go away
Still coming along the floor
That it it's time for war.

Its little black legs are dark as night
Running along like a wolf who needs his food
Fangs begin to appear, oh no it's my worst fear!

Danielle Maslin (12)
Windsor High School

GRAVEYARDS

As I wandered in the eerie graveyard,
Shadows appeared in my imagination,
I feel jumpy and unsettled,
The graves seem humungous,
The names on the graves seem unusual,
In this creepy, deserted place!

Charlotte Perry (12)
Windsor High School

THE DARK

The room is dark,
I am all alone!
The house is still
Everyone seems to be in a deep sleep.

Shadows cast over me
The clock ticks,
All the toys seem to come to life
Walking like zombies towards me.

I switch on my light!
Everything is normal,
Toys are still and quiet
Until I turn out the light.

Morning has broken
The sun lights up the sky
The dark seems to run and hide!
Until night, then it comes back again.

Christopher Whiley (12)
Windsor High School

THE *IT* BEHIND YOU

I was walking along just minding my own business
when *it* appeared behind me,
moving and curling, copying my every move.

Suddenly *it's* gone,
I do not know where it is lurking,
watching me, staring at me.

There *it* is, back again,
pointing, laughing,
I think I will walk away.

It goes again,
I know that *it* won't return,
stupid, afraid of my own shadow.

Sara Griffiths (13)
Windsor High School

SNAKE

Slithering, sinuous, shining,
The snake sidled amongst the grasses.
Its eyes were sinisterly staring,
Staring at me.

Frenzied, forked, flickering,
The snake's tongue flashed in and out.
Its tongue was motioning,
Motioning, 'Follow me.'

Bold, barbed, brazen,
The snake bared its fangs,
Its fangs were showing mercilessly,
Mercilessly at me.

Petrified, panicked, passing out,
I stood frozen to the spot.
I freaked and ran,
I turned and it was gone.

Harry Dunbar (12)
Windsor High School

HEIGHTS

Your palms start to sweat,
Your legs and arms stiffen,
Your whole body turns into a statue,
You become speechless
As you gasp for breath.
You look down.

You know you shouldn't have,
But the temptation was too great.
You start to tremble,
Your legs turn to jelly,
You get cramp in your feet,
But you're too scared to feel it.

I close my eyes and walk away,
I'm no longer at a height,
But my heart's still pounding.
It's pounding like I've just done 50 laps of a football pitch,
I'm still trembling like I've had a near death experience,
Well to me it was!

Joshua McBain (12)
Windsor High School

GHOSTS

G hosts are prehistoric,
H orrifying and blood freezing,
O ld houses are where they linger, linger, linger,
S pindly stairs are where they float, float, float,
T hey give chills up people's spines,
S caring them to death.

Amy Masters (12)
Windsor High School

HALLOWE'EN

Hallowe'en, Hallowe'en,
What a scary scene,
Ghouls and ghosts,
I can smell cheese on toast.
Lots of treats,
Some are sweets,
It's dark about,
Children shout,
Are you in for a fright
Tonight.
Midnight comes,
The children go home,
All alone.

Lisa White (12)
Windsor High School

SPIDERS

They're creepy and they're crawly,
They're hairy and appalling,

They like to live in baths,
Do they come down the taps?

I creep into the shower
And look up to my horror.

An eight legged creature,
Looking down at me.

I think to myself I'm not that dirty,
I'll have one tomorrow.

Rebecca Lloyd (12)
Windsor High School

IN THE DARK

Scared, betrayed, lonely,
In the dark,
I felt a shiver go down my spine,
As my mouth started to quiver.

Afraid, left alone, tired,
I started to calm myself down,
Until the light started to flicker
And the curtains started to move.

The moonlight shone through the gaps,
Making darting shadows on the wall,
Howling noises were coming from everywhere,
I heard noises in my ears.

The eerie sound of silence did not seem quiet anymore.

Liam Pawlowski (12)
Windsor High School

THE GRAVEYARD

I walked cautiously into the eerie silence,
My shadow cast upon the trees
Which swayed in the moonlit air,
Grey gravestones seemed to light up as I passed,
A shiver ran up my spine,
The cold night air chilled my bones,
Alone in the deep dark night,
A mist seemed to cover everything,
In the lonesome graveyard!

Kimberley Horne (12)
Windsor High School

CREEPY CRAWLY SPIDERS

Creepy-crawly spiders
Creeping everywhere
With their fat hairy bodies
They give us all a scare

On the walls they climb
On the floors they glide
Scurrying for cover in a hope to hide.

Creepy-crawly spiders
Creeping everywhere
I hate the really big ones
That seem to stop and glare.

Lara Kuczerawy (12)
Windsor High School

NIGHTMARES

I screamed and ran for my life,
I'm being followed, I screamed at the top
of my voice.
The bullet was fired,
it came closer.
'Noooooo!' I screamed
'Wake up.'
I opened my eyes.
'Did they catch him?'
I asked.
That nightmare bugged me
every other night in my life.

David Hayward (12)
Windsor High School

Ghosts, Ghouls And Graveyards

Spooky tombstones, dismal furnishings,
Startling gravestones and petrifying spirits.
The disobedient ghosts and ghouls
Horrendously flew out of the worn away graves.

I froze with fear and wanted to scream,
My teeth were tingled to the gums
And my bones were chilled to the end
But the rest of me was haunted.

It was 12 o'clock at night
And I was walking through a graveyard.
Suddenly I slipped over
And fell into a grave through a hole.

I tried to climb up but I fell
And landed on a coffin.
I then knew that this was bad luck,
The walls were gloomy and dull.

I opened up the engraved coffin,
It was pitch black and I could not see.
I stepped inside the coffin but I landed on my bed
Next to a coffin engraved
Daniel Fisher (1986-1999)
Aged 12
RIP

Daniel Fisher (12)
Windsor High School

TIGERS

A tiger is my favourite cat,
So graceful in its habitat.
Tigers love water and splash in it for hours
Then lie in the sunlight and roll in the flowers.
I love tigers, they're the best,
Siberian, Bengal and the rest.
They have sharp teeth and sharp claws,
They have big whiskers and big paws.
They started off as sabretooths,
With fangs twenty centimetres and that's the truth.
They can weigh as much as three hundred and eighty kilograms,
That's over five times the weight of two grown lambs.
They live to fifteen in the wild,
And about twenty away from the wild.
So a tiger is different than what you thought,
So let's all try and stop them from being caught.

Louise Bishop (13)
Windsor High School

NIGHTMARES

I lie awake in my bed
Not wanting to close my eyes and sleep.
I cringe when I think about nightmares
I lie in my bed and start to weep.
My eyes start to close
Into dreamland I go
Paralysed as I dream, my whole body dead and stiff.
This is a nightmare, I'm being chased, chased,
Aaahhh.

Hayley Bird (12)
Windsor High School

DID YOU GET THEM?

'Yes, I have,'
'Yippee, now we can go.'
It was the big match day,
I got my scarf and shirt and got in the car,
We parked the car and I could hear loud cheers,
We gave in our tickets
Then went for some food.
I walked up the big steps,
The crowd cheered.
Soon the big game started,
First we scored,
Then again,
Soon the away team scored four!
Our heads sunk into our hands,
The ref blew the final whistle.
Boos came from all round the ground.
The away team had won.
'I hate Tottenham,' I said,
'I still have faith in West Bromwich Albion though.'

Mark Walton (12)
Windsor High School

POLLY, POLLY PRETTY DOLLY

I lay in my bed about to fall asleep,
Then I turned my head,
Two blue eyes stared lifelessly at me,
It was lurking amongst the shadows.
The ghostly figure moved swiftly,
I wanted to run, run away,
But my body froze with fear,
I felt helpless, lonely and nervous.

The evil cackle I had heard so many times before,
Filled the room once more,
I was frantic, shaking in my bed,
Images moved around the room,
I put my head under my pillow,
But my phobia didn't go away
I felt something ice-cold touch my back,

I knew deep in my soul I wasn't alone . . .

Emma Reeve (12)
Windsor High School

THE PC

Push the button, turn it on,
Here it comes, the information bomb!
Games, reference, Internet and more,
The heart of technology under your nose!

Half life, FIFA 99, and The Phantom Menace
Are among the games that feature on the computer,
Suddenly you're overflowed with data,
I'm going on the Internet later!

Computer storage space is measured in bytes,
Memory is measured in RAM,
Monitor resolution is measured in pixels
And the speed of the computer is measured in Hertz.

In the PC World there are many top brands,
Mesh, Tiny, Time are all included
To make computers best for using,
Computers are ace, computers are cool,
Get one now, they're the ultimate tool!

Andy Patterson (13)
Windsor High School

NIGHTMARES

Have you ever had a dream that was so frightening
you woke up in a cold sweat?
I have.
What did it involve?
Ghosts, vampires, dragons?
Mine did.
When you woke up after the nightmare had ended
could you still see the scary faces every time you
closed your eyes?
I could.
In the morning, could you remember the nightmare?
I could.
Did you tell anyone?
I did.

Daniel Franklin (13)
Windsor High School

GRAVEYARDS AND NIGHTMARES

Dark, creepy, eerie,
I looked round,
I saw thousands of graves.
Cold, damp, terrified,
The night was black,
The moon shone,
Alone, scared, anxious,
I turned round,
A ghost,
Looking for me,
I woke up.

Elliot Freeth (12)
Windsor High School

HAMMY THE HAMSTER ESCAPES

So Hammy the Hamster decided
His house in the kitchen was poor,
At the first chance that hit,
He would pack up his kit
And leave with a view to explore.

One night to his joy and amazement,
The roof of his house disappeared,
So he bundled up his bed
And the food on which he fed,
And left the house totally cleared.

He travelled around in the darkness,
He looked and he checked this and that,
But knowing what was best
He stopped for a rest,
And settled for his own basement flat!

Claire Hartshorne (13)
Windsor High School

NIGHTMARES!

Dripping with cold sweat,
Shivering and scared,
The dream seemed real.
Trembling, shaking with terror,
Monsters and scary things,
Blood freezing, bone-shaking fear,
Hearing things that bump in the night,
Wondering will it ever go away.

Hannah Woodward (13)
Windsor High School

MY WEEK

Monday is the start of the week
        And I'm feeling rather bleak.
Tuesday is football magazine day
        While I'm dreaming of being on a bay.
Wednesday comes rather quick
        I've had enough of my dad taking the mick.
Thursday and the week's nearly done
        Soon it will be the weekend and I'll have some fun.
Friday's here and school's out,
        It's time to scream and shout!
Saturday's here, football's on,
        Let's see if Villa's won.
Sunday is the day of rest
        Before I restart my schooling quest.

Adam Clarke (13)
Windsor High School

SPIDER!

I was sitting calm and content.
Out of nowhere
Came a spider!
Creeping in from under the fireplace,
Big, bulky, bulbous body.
Eight beady eyes silently looking at me,
Long hairy legs twitching,
Now I'm frightened and nervous,
What will it do next?
Then as fast as lightning
It's gone.

Sarah Taylor (12)
Windsor High School

RACEHORSE

My favourite animal is a horse,
I was so excited when I went to the racecourse,
There were so many horses everywhere,
A flood of silky, flowing hair.

There were chestnuts, browns, blacks and bays
But I fell in love with a sweet dappled grey.
There it danced and pranced around,
Nervously lifting its hoof and pawing the ground.

Its head was up and its tail was high,
Trying to follow the other horses that galloped by,
It snorted and lunged away to the right,
The poor stable boy held on oh so tight.

But the grey was strong and full of power,
The stablehand did nothing but stand and cower,
The horse reared and backed away,
Before galloping off with a triumphant neigh.

I stood still, my eyes were glued to the grey,
While other people ran to get out of its way,
Its muscles were flexed and its hooves were pounding,
Up the finishing straight the runaway horse bounded.

Its nostrils were flared, snorting out puffs of determination
Those deep, brown eyes showing a look of domination.
The wind brushed its hair back with such a force,
Oh my beautiful, elegant racehorse.

Kelly Marshall (13)
Windsor High School

AFRAID

Every night when I fall asleep,
I dream the same dream.
I'm on top of a cliff looking down,
There's no one else around.
I try to move myself away,
But that proves difficult.
I can't move an inch let alone a mile,
Paralysed with fear.
There's something about that very place,
That beckons me each night.
Calling me, mocking me, saying I'm afraid,
Afraid of that deserted place.

As I'm looking down,
Deep into that pit of rocks,
A wave of fright washes over me.
I know what's going to happen next,
It happens every time.
My feet crawl slowly forward,
I feel giddy as I reach the edge.
Unable to look anymore, I topple over,
Somersaulting into the air.
As I'm plunging to my death,
Deep in a pit of rocks,
Falling, falling, falling, falling,
As if I'd never stop.
The rocks come nearer,
I can feel them already
My body hitting them,
Sounding like eggs cracking

I can hear it already,
It's almost real,
But before I hit the bottom,
I wake up in a cold sweat,
Hearing the sound, *crrack*
Over and over again.

Holly Fowkes (12)
Windsor High School

SHAKESPEARE'S TALE

Two small days in fair Verona
Told a tale for lives hereafter.
Juliet and Romeo
Fell in love, didst thou know?

An ancient grudge,
A death marked love,
Two serious foes
Spelt serious woes.

How can I tell
How they both felt?
What can I say
To make the sadness go away?

What will be, will be,
Is what they said,
Now we know,
Because they're both dead.

Two deaths marked
Loves' finest hour.
Tybalt resides in hell,
All this Shakespeare tells.

Heather Buttery (13)
Windsor High School

THERE'S NO FREEDOM FOR ME!

I'm an Asian elephant,
You can see me in the circus,
You can see me in the zoo,
You can see me in the wild,
If I'm around to see you.
Hunters kill me for my tusks
By shooting from up high,
Then they
Gas me,
Strangle me,
Trap me,
Electrocute me,
What do they want from me?
They want my tusks for ivory
So they can trade it in,
What will they do when there's none left of me?
I just want to be free,
But there's no freedom for me.

Rebecca Down (13)
Windsor High School

THEM

They have hairy, black bodies and long, thin legs,
They spin their webs, minding their own business,
Yet they cause so much trouble.
To look at them sends shivers down your spine,
An awful sick feeling in the pit of your stomach,
You just want to scream and scream.
The light, tickly feeling as they crawl all over you.
They can be called Money, or Garden, or House.
Can you guess who 'They' are?

Lisa Cooper (12)
Windsor High School

LOVE

Love is a word that comes and goes
But do people really know
What it means to love somebody
The tears may fade away
I'm so glad his love can stay
Because I love him
And he'll show me what it really means to love.

Chanelle Richards (12)
Windsor High School

SNOWFLAKES

Falling, falling, falling,
Being released from the sky,
Then hitting the ground,
Not making a sound,
They slowly melt away.

Lucy Follis (13)
Windsor High School

AUTUMN LEAVES

Autumn splendour on the trees,
Gently falling in the breeze,
Leaves of golden brown, so mellow,
Orange, purple, red and yellow.
When nature's carpet is on the floor,
Summer days will be no more!

Daniel Jones (12)
Windsor High School

THE FLICKS

We sit in folding chairs
And begin to watch adverts,
We think of the reviews
And reports we may have heard.

We munch away at popcorn
And rustle sweet wrappers
Then the lights dim down
And we all fall to silence.

Sound blasts through the speakers,
Light gleams from the screen
And production introductions begin
For something we have not seen.

We stop in our actions
And settle right down,
For we're here for the next few hours,
The film is rolling now!

Chris Stevenson (13)
Windsor High School

SLEEPY WORM!

There's a long, long worm a-crawling
across the roof of my tent.
I can hear the whistle blowing,
and it's time I went.

That worm, he was a nuisance
because he spoilt my morning dip.
When I returned I found this worm
Upon my pillowslip.

Kayleigh Endres (13)
Windsor High School

BILLIONS OF EMOTIONS AND ONLY 24 HOURS IN A DAY

One more day,
What to say,
Angry, mad or sad?
All these emotions, I just can't cope.
They're making me feel bad.

More emotions every day,
Learning to cope in every way.
Listen to people and what they say,
Getting through life day by day.

Days feel long, although they're short,
Life's not really what I thought,
People laugh and people cry,
People live and people die.

Rachel Adams (13)
Windsor High School

AUTUMN DAYS

Dry, crinkly leaves are all around,
Red, orange, yellow and brown.
The long, hot summer days are no more,
Sunbathing just a memory.

An autumn chill greets my nose,
I must get out my warm clothes.
Oh why did summer say goodbye,
And take away the beautiful, blue sky?

Jessica Solomon (13)
Windsor High School

POEM

I was walking in the forest one day
When I came across a monster
The monster was as big as a tree,
I hoped he hadn't seen me.
I froze like a startled rabbit in a headlight
And with leaded feet I couldn't run out of sight,
The monster was as hairy as a gorilla,
Like the monsters are in thrillers.
He spat like a camel
And smelt like a pig,
He stood as tall as an oil rig.
He circled round me like a swarm of bees,
The pain brought me to my knees.
As I recoiled like a snake I felt as if the earth might shake,
But as I lay there quivering like a jelly,
He gently placed me on his belly.
I looked into his big, blue eyes,
They looked like stars in the skies,
He looked at me and said,
'Will you come play with me?'

Nicola Atterbury (13)
Windsor High School

I CAN'T WRITE POEMS

I can't write poems,
I don't know why,
It's not my fault,
But here I try!

Martyn Morris (13)
Windsor High School

BUSTER

I have a rabbit and he's called Buster,
He is so naughty he gets me in a fluster.
His glistening fur waves in the breeze,
He's very nosy, he likes to jump up my knees.

He's affectionate and very loyal,
Full of mischief and acts as if he's royal!
Gobbling up all his food,
Slobbering and munching, he's very rude!

His little tail bobs up and down,
Dives and races everywhere like a clown,
Once he jumped into my female rabbit's cage,
And I went into a rage.

He cowered in the corner looking very smug,
And then I forgave him and gave him a hug,
I can't wait because . . . she's pregnant.

Laura Smith (13)
Windsor High School

FUR

A nimals die from terrible torture,
N ever to see daylight again,
I t must be stopped,
M ammals may become extinct,
A nd whales and dolphins die,
L ife will fade away. Why?

F ur is for cold-hearted people,
U nless something is done,
R ight away, life will be at loss.

Sara Evans (13)
Windsor High School

RUGBY

Rugby is my favourite game,
I love to play it in the rain.
Someone starts to come down the line,
I tackle them in the nick of time.

I grab the ball as fast as I can,
With quick thinking I pass it to Dan.
He runs until he is nearly there,
I shout 'Pass it back, there's no time to spare.'

Running frantically, not much time,
But oh no, look it's there, number nine.
Crash, bang, a great big thud,
All confused, there I stood.

I looked at my hands, I still had the ball,
Just one man left, but about 30 metres tall.
I felt like I could barely crawl,
But then I thought 'Could I score?'

I was on my own, with the ball in my hands,
One by one the whole crowd stands,
Then I dived straight over the line,
Try scored and victory is mine!

Arron Clifford (13)
Windsor High School

WHAT IF IT WAS YOU?

Bullfight, bullfight,
come and get your ticket,
Watch a defenceless bull get tortured,
Bring your vaseline along,
We'll smear it in its eyes,
Blind him, torture him . . .
Kill him if we can.

So what, as you say?
Fifteen pounds to watch the bullfight
And twenty for his meat!
Well I say, instead of it being the bull . . .
What if it was you?

Rebecca Rudge (13)
Windsor High School

IN THE WOODS

Dare you go in the wood
in the night
to get a fright?
Anyone who dares to go
in the wood tonight,
what a sight.
What is there, no one knows,
no one except the crows.
They chirp and sing cries of alarm
as something fiercely grabs your arm.
You scream and shout
but no one hears,
as you shake with so much fear.
He reveals himself from his hide,
with blood coming from his side.
You notice it's just a kitten
and its side has been bitten.
You take it home, you love it so,
you call the little kitten Joe.

Jessica Priest (13)
Windsor High School

SUNDAYS

There's nothing to do
and nothing to say,
nowhere to go
and nowhere to play.

The shops are all closed
and the High Street is dead,
I walk all alone,
silence going to my head.

My friends have all left me,
gone off on their own,
I'm getting so bored now
I think I'll go home.

It's starting to rain,
I get wetter and wetter,
what else could go wrong?
Maybe tomorrow will be better.

Michelle Emery (13)
Windsor High School

IF I WAS . . .

If I was a conductor
Of a big orchestra,
I'd make them play extra fast!
That would make them suffer!

If I was an astronomer
Gazing up at night,
I'd blow up another planet,
That would be a sight!

If I was a film director,
Rolling around in dosh,
I'd make a scary horror film,
Never caring about the cost!

If I was in a pop band,
I'd write funny lyrics,
Add a funny tune too
So everyone would be in hysterics!

James Elias (13)
Windsor High School

DO THEY THINK . . .

Do they think it's fair
to desert a hare,
or to be cruel to me?

Do they think it's right
that I put up a fight
when they try to send me to sleep?

Do they think it's fine,
do we tow the line
while we're sitting here half dead?

But would they think it's fair
if it weren't on a hare,
but on them, sitting here half dead?

Rachael Rossiter (13)
Windsor High School

THE FUTURISTIC MILLENNIUM

The new millennium's nearly here,
I wonder if anyone will show a surprised tear?

There will be celebrations all night long,
People will have a laugh and sing a jolly song.

This millennium seems all dirty and old,
Will the new be bright and bold?

Will it be fun and bright?
Or will there be more battles and fights?

I wonder what the new millennium will be like?
Will we be riding on electric bikes?

Will we still have to go to school?
Or will computer's be our educational tools?

I wonder will we still use cars?
And will we be able to fly to Mars?

Paul Luckett (13)
Windsor High School

WAR

Bang, bang, bang, gunshots echo in the night sky,
Thud, thud, thud, the artillery pummels the enemy lines,
Thud, thud, thud, my heart imitates the tools of war.
Argghh - the scream of a wasted life,
Bang, bang, bang, the light from the muzzles of guns illuminates us,
Flash of light like spectres of the innocent,
Argghh - the wail of a ghost to be.

Stuart Land (13)
Windsor High School

THE BARBARIC SLAUGHTER

Is it right or is it not
To kill animals to help us?
Many are killed every day
And some of these do not help much!

'How would you like your fur, Madam,
Trapped, gassed or strangled?'
'Excuse me, assistant, you see this rug,
It looks like a bear . . . all *mangled!*'

So going back to the question I posed,
Is it right or is it not?
I mean vivisection, the harming of animals,
And does it help us a lot?

Vaccines and cures have been tested
And some of those have helped,
But some of them have done no good,
And have never seen the shelf!

So, the barbaric slaughter is doing okay,
But not so good as well,
So should it carry on like this
Putting animals through such hell?

Or should it be stopped, and the animals freed
And the practitioners court martialled and killed
And should we made do with what we already have,
Medicines, vaccines and pills?

It's up to you, the people of Earth,
And the next generations too.
But for now it'll go on in its barbaric ways
With these animals, *pointlessly*, killed.

Daniel Richards (13)
Windsor High School

VIVISECTION

V   ivisection is torture to animals,
I   t has to stop,
V   ery innocent animals are being killed for no reason,
I   f it doesn't stop, some animals will become extinct.
S   cientists believe that it is for our own good,
E   ven if it means killing many animals,.
C   ats are a prime example of animals which are used
                                   for experiments.
T   hese experiments are never explained to us.
I   f they were explained, we could understand why they
                                kill these animals.
O   n a good note, vivisection has saved the lives of half a
                         million people. Even so, still say
N   o.

Simon Howell (13)
Windsor High School

VIVISECTION

V   ile and horrible,
I   ndecent and nasty,
V   ivisection is cruel.
I   n labs and bunkers,
S   ecret tests on animals,
E   verything is hurt, nothing is spared,
C   ats and dogs,
T   urtles and monkeys,
I   n pain,
O   n tables,
N   o hope.

Ben Smith (13)
Windsor High School

IT'S A HARD LIFE

All day long in the boiling sun,
The donkey rides on and on.

Back and forth from sea to shore
While he's thinking, 'Please no more.'

People on his back, walking up and down,
On the beach around and around.

Carrying people for the money,
But he does not think it's all that funny.

At the end of the day he's all worn out,
Then he hears someone shout

'Come on donkey, stand on those legs,
You've got to do it all again.'

Victoria Page (13)
Windsor High School

VIVISECTION

V   ery scary,
I   ncreasingly cramped,
V   arious implements of torture,
I   will soon be tested,
S   oon I will go,
E   bbing away is my life,
C   urious about what they will do,
T   housands of volts going through my neck,
I   feel like I'm going to die,
O   nly then do they stop,
N   ow I'm crippled, left to die.

Thomas Hackett (13)
Windsor High School

THE BLUEBIRD OF UNHAPPINESS

I feel the rain bristling on my neck, every day, even in summer.
The cold bites on my fingers, gripping tightly, it won't let go.
In my head I'm saying, 'Everything I've ever done for this person.'

Occasionally I think 'If this is bad, how do the starving, the poor
and the sick feel?'
This is a point of unhappiness no one ever looks at.

I try so hard to challenge his opinion.
I try so hard to please him, and yet I don't even want to.
Yes, we do laugh and no, I'm not an unhappy person.

There are many other people who I can talk to, just not him.

I feel slightly sad because someone occasionally makes me sad.
The rest of the world's poverty-stricken people have a lifetime
of unhappiness.
It just goes to show what self-sympathetic people are worth.

I never think, 'Am I dreaming, will I wake up to the sun,'
I wake up thinking, 'The same place, the same time, the same day
and the same person.'
Sometimes it's a good thing, sometimes (mostly), it's a bad thing.
I try thinking, starvation . . . poverty . . .
I or nobody else could imagine this poverty.
I as one person am lucky.
He as one person is lucky.

James Hampton (13)
Windsor High School

THE LIFE OF HE

He pulls the children on his back
All day long,
In the boiling, boiling hot,
With no water that he can drink.

Round and round the same way,
Feeling sore and sad,
He does not know a better life,
That is good, not bad.

Nobody treats him with care
Or takes his feelings in,
He does long for some loving fuss
But all he gets is a smack on his back.

What is he doing all day long
Into a life of doom?
He is a carousel horse of course,
So now you see what the life is like
Of He.

Becky Crowther (13)
Windsor High School

CHRISTMAS

You wake up on Christmas morning,
All excited but still yawning,
Wondering what's in the shiny paper,
Then all revealed a few minutes later,
The tinsel glitters on the tree,
The lights twinkle for all to see,
Then all the excitement has passed away,
But family and friends are here to stay.

Rachel Oakley (12)
Windsor High School

In The Future

Robots, spaceships, visits to Mars,
Walk on the clouds and fly to the stars.
Cures for diseases and new medicines too,
The sea will turn yellow and the grass will turn blue.
Virtual reality's just one of those things,
Every single baby born will have a pair of golden wings,
There will also be time travel to take you to the past,
To find out ancient history and mysteries at last.
Skyboards not skateboards and jet-powered rollerblades,
More communication to planets for the trades.
Aliens living on Earth from outer space,
What will have happened? Its not just the human race!
Computers will take over, there'll be nothing left to do,
No work, no war, no illness, it'll be a perfect world for you!

Kate Currier (13)
Windsor High School

My Nan Is A Sumo Wrestler

Did you know my nan is a sumo wrestler,
She can bend a big steal bar in two?
Did you know if everyone picks on me, she will get them.
Did you know my nan is a sumo wrestler?
She can pick up a car with people in,
Did you know she rides a Harley Davidson?
(Now how cool is that?)
Did you know my nan is a sumo wrestler?
She can beat up 12 gangsters,
Did you know she's the best nan in the whole wide world?

Alex Wagstaff (11)
Windsor High School

ANIMAL CRUELTY

A nimals suffer,
N ot humans,
I gnorant vivisectionists,
M ake animals surgical toys,
A nimals are helpless against them,
L ying virtually unconscious.

C ats, guinea pigs, mice and
R ats are walking experiments,
U sually they die young,
E ven babies are used,
L ittle, white, adorable kittens,
T ry to battle their way through life,
Y elping like many other animals for their lives.

James Goodwin (13)
Windsor High School

MOON

I have a white cat whose name is Moon,
He eats catfish from a wooden spoon
And sleeps till five each afternoon.

Moon goes out when the moon is bright
And sycamore trees are spotted white
To sit and stare in the dead of night.

Beyond still water cries a tragic loon,
Through mulberry leaves, peers a wild baboon
And in Moon's eyes I see a moon.

Amy Au (13)
Windsor High School

INNOCENT

Staring through the bars I think:
'What have I done wrong?
Robbed a bank maybe,
Or stolen some rare diamond?
No, I am innocent.

But still I sit in solitary confinement,
Alone and scared,
Waiting to see what they
Will do to me today.
Torture me maybe,
Or spray something in my eyes
So I am blinded?

But why?
Why do I need to be put through this,
To feel that death is better than staying alive?
So some human can wear eyeshadow,
Or get rid of a tiny headache?
After all, humans are better than us.
They maim, blind, torture and kill,
But still we should respect them.

So I will sit here
And endure this pain until I am thrown aside,
No longer needed
And vivisection has claimed another life.

Ella Reid-Norris (13)
Windsor High School

MILLENNIUM

Whizz, whoopee,
It's here today,
Millennium 2000,
I'm here to say,
Happy New Year
In a special way.

Millennium Bug
Please beware,
This creepy-crawly
Will give you a scare,
Down it, down it,
What a dare.

Champagne, bubbly,
Drinks galore,
In the morning
You'll feel a bit sore.
Don't drink and drive
You're breaking the law.

Whizz, whoopee,
It's here today,
Millennium 2000,
I'm here to say.
Happy New Year
In a special way!

Chris Knowles (13)
Windsor High School

THE WOMAN, THE WITCH AND THE MOUSE

There is a woman who lives next door,
she lives at number 34.
I went round to her house the other day
and surprisingly enough, it was her birthday.
It was very strange when I was round at her house,
you see there was this black and white mouse,
when I sat down it started to twitch,
then with a puff of smoke, it turned into a witch.
I turned around and the woman had gone,
there on the seat was a vol-au-vent,
I turned around and looked quite shocked,
the witch just laughed and then she flew off.
I stood up, I couldn't believe my eyes,
then the vol-au-vent spoke, 'Help me,' it cried.
There was a tap, tap, tap on the door,
it was the woman who lived at number 34.
'Excuse me, what are you doing here?' she asked,
'I thought I could pop in as I passed.'
'Sit down, I'll make us some tea,
would you like a vol-au-vent with me?'
I answered with a cool 'No, thank you,'
and shot out of the house,
I ran round to my house and had a cup of tea,
I felt very calm after this, with the added brandy.

Emma Chamberlain (13)
Windsor High School

SCHOOL TIME

School can be boring,
School can be fun.
I go in the morning,
Driven by my mum.

We have to take books,
Talk and get into trouble.
The wild teacher looks cross
If your gum blows a bubble.

Alexander Powis (11)
Windsor High School

VIVISECTION - GOOD OR BAD

Polio, Leprosy, Malaria, AIDS, Typhoid, Cancer,
Tumours, blindness, Leukaemia, Meningitis, Dementia,
Cystic Fibrosis, Sickle Cell Anaemia, Parkinson's.

They cause us suffering and bring us pain,
I know my life is starting to wane.

They are respecters of no one, young, old, or even unborn,
They are bringers of grief and leave you forlorn.

The death toll is endless, there's no end to the plight,
We must make amends to continue the fight.

To end all this misery there must be research,
Please don't leave those who suffer in the lurch.

Do everything possible in your power
To eradicate diseases, hour by hour.

Donor cards give people a chance,
So don't stand back, take a stance.

Everything possible under the sun
To save a life must be done.

Remedies and cures are far too few,
So medical advancement must include vivisection too.

Tony Boffey (13)
Windsor High School

Year 2000

From now 'til then, not too long,
Just think what's happened,
War, death, tragedy,
There once was Elvis and The Beatles,
Now there's Boyzone and Backstreet Boys.

Some could say time has flown,
What will happen? Will the world still spin?
Computers exploding, machines stop working and dogs
                                        quit barking.
What's all the fuss about?

The time is near,
For a new millennium,
What will it mean? How will life be?
Who knows?

Many have been born, many died,
We've all mourned the tragic loss of Princess Diana,
And praised the inventions we couldn't live without,
but is the millennium worth all the fuss?

Then the world is really noisy,
I cant hear a thing,
Not long to go,
The world will be silent.

Millennium, it's finally here,
Poppers popping, people screaming,
The Millennium Dome is an amazing sight,
Fireworks everywhere in the sky.

Is this an invitation for the unwelcome ghostly, ghouls?
And will the millennium be all we expect?
Will it be good or will it be bad?
We'll just have to wait and see!

Sarah Walton (13)
Windsor High School

MY BEST FRIEND

My best friend's a boozer,
Doesn't give a damn,
Whisky, scotch and vodka,
Drinks whatever she can.

My best friend's a druggie,
Doesn't really care,
Takes Ecstasy, smokes pot and speed
It doesn't matter where.

My best friend's a smoker,
Doesn't think it's wrong,
Smokes in school and won't give up,
Been doing it so long.

My best friend's bulimic,
Doesn't think it's bad,
She eats so much then throws it up,
Her case is really sad.

But my best friend's a laugh,
There's not much there to hate,
You can say her life's messed up,
But she's a really smashing mate.

Carrie Macklin (13)
Windsor High School

THE KITTEN

'Free to good homes.'
Six pretty kittens
All colours under the rainbow.
Please, will you choose one?

Sightless, multicoloured balls of fluff,
Mewing, scrambling, lying together.
One stood up and moved closer.
Please, will you choose me?

A cute kitten, eyes like amber;
Tortoiseshell, with four white paws,
Climbing over her siblings,
Please, will you take me?

Home in a borrowed basket
To a strange bed and scratching post.
New people, new smells, new house,
Thank you, for choosing me.

Ben Parkes (13)
Windsor High School

AUTUMN LEAVES

It's autumn time again,
A time when leaves fall to the ground,
Golden brown and russet red
Replace the healthy green
That should be instead.
A new, thick carpet of
Dead leaves is formed,
Be it in the park or on your lawn.
It's autumn time again.

Shelley Hardy (13)
Windsor High School

THE LIFE OF A THIRTEEN-YEAR-OLD

Boxed in, tempers flare,
I argue with my parents,
When you're thirteen, you're always wrong.

There's no one to talk to,
No support,
I sound stressed? I suppose I am.

Stressed? They screech,
At thirteen you have no problems,
Wait until the real world, you'll see.

Depressed - that's the word,
We all feel it,
Though it stays with some longer than others.

Friendships can be difficult,
Relationships, up and down,
Pressure to do well in life.

Expectations can get you down,
Moods are hard to cope with,
Peer pressure surrounds us.

Smoking, drugs and drinking,
Bullying, truancy and violence,
How can you not get involved?

It's all so difficult,
Hard to cope,
Impossible not to think 'What's the point?'

My life keeps going
The world keeps spinning,
They say I'm not alone,
So why do I feel like I am?

Hannah Tibbetts (13)
Windsor High School

IN WONDERLAND

In Wonderland
Something had begun,
The moonlight shone,
The fairies danced,
Merry men clapped their hands.

I don't believe it
When people say
In that land far away
Where fairies play
And people sleep,
Deep beneath the jungle heat.

Where witches live
And goblins sing,
Where elephants chill beneath the sea,
It's a grand place to be.

In Wonderland
Something's begun,
Something fun for everyone,
I still remember to this day
The beauty of that land far away.

Rachael Bull (13)
Windsor High School

TIME

T ick-tock, tick-tock goes the clock,
I   mmortally goes the world.
M illennium the year 2000
E nding of the nineteen hundreds.

Hannah Bissell (11)
Windsor High School

FEELINGS

Sad, lonely and melancholy
Happiness, eagerness and elation
Hate, hostility and detestation
Heartbroken
Grievous and crushed
Feverish feelings are writhing inside my body
Evolving every breathing moment
Hurt, pain and devastation
Anger, rage and infuriation
Love,
Passion,
And warmth.

My heart pours out many emotions
All as immense as vast, almighty oceans.

Rhian Banks (13)
Windsor High School

CHRISTMAS

C hestnuts falling from the trees,
H itting everybody's knees,
R udolf is coming to eat his carrots,
I n a box of mouldy parrots,
S anta, Santa hurry up and come,
T ime is passing and I'm going dumb,
M y mum says 'It wants to be soon'
A s I'm blowing up a balloon,
S anta's going, going gone, I looked again
                    he's just like Mom!

Jack Willmott (11)
Windsor High School

MY TRUE NORTH

With the North Star
You always know where you are,
When I'm lost you're always there,
To dry my tears when I cry.
When I really need a friend,
To talk to,
To laugh with,
To share a secret,
To sigh over lost loves,
You're always there.
With the North Star,
You always know where you are,
You are my true north.

Jodie Horrobin (13)
Windsor High School

DREAM

I have a dream
It was a dream about
Dracula
He was after me
He was trying to kill me
I was running and running but I
Wasn't fast enough to get away from him
He was gaining on me angry
Angry and thirsty for my blood
He caught me I was struggling
He let go, I hid. He
Didn't see me again
I have a bad dream.
Dream.

Sam Carter (11)
Windsor High School

THE WEATHERMAN

Storms are frightening
Electric, lightning
Hurricane roaring,
Debris soaring
Destroying.

Sun scorching
Blazing, torching
Tornado wrecking
Danger beckoning
Threatening
Rain flooding
Hale bouncing
Blizzard whirling
Snow twirling
Swirling.

I blame it on the weatherman!

Paul Campbell (13)
Windsor High School

I'M A GREYHOUND

I'm a greyhound, watch me run,
Twist and turn, have some fun,
Chasing the hare round and round,
I love to run, I love the sound,
I'm 38 kilos, pound, pound, pound,
First place here I come,
Hooray now at last I've won.

Amy Finch (13)
Windsor High School

THE GREY MARE

Galloping through the fields was a striking grey mare,
Her long, silky, flowing mane streaming through the air.

Her beautiful dished, pretty face,
Showing off her stature elegance and grace.

Her nostrils were flared, her neck was arched,
Over the field the grey mare marched.

Her sparkling hooves drumming out a pattern,
Her shiny glistening coat, as soft as satin.

A look of intelligence and warmth in her eyes,
Around the field, the grey mare flies.

Leanne Townsend (13)
Windsor High School

HALLOWE'EN

I like to dress up spooky
And go trick or treating
My mask is a devil
I took it off my brother
My costume was all red
And I made a fork as well
I walked out the door
Knocked.on another door
Trick or treat
Give me sweets.

Julie Crumpton (11)
Windsor High School

WHEN I'M OLDER

When I'm older, (I'm only 5)
I'm going to be Superman.
I'll use special powers on my sister,
She'll be my servant
And make my breakfast
And she will do the washing up
And make the beds.

(2 days later)
When I'm older, (I'm only 5)
I'm going to fly a plane
I'll do stunts for my friends,
They'll be so pleased I took them up
They will buy me pressies
And will really like me
And I'll do it for them again and again.

(2 days later)
When I'm older, (I'm only 5)
I'm going to be a policeman.
I'll boss all the bad guys around
They'll never be bad guys again
And they'll become policemen
And boss other bad guys around
And make them not bad.

Adam Sankey (12)
Windsor High School

A Doggy Tail

Paul has a dog, his name is Fred,
It thinks it's clever in the head.
It could have won a Noble prize,
If he wasn't in a doggy disguise.

Paul had been heard to mutter
'I want an ordinary dog.'
Not a clever scholar.

Paul's dog does not get on well with other dogs.
He thinks they are rather thick,
He just sits at his computer,
While they are chasing sticks.

Paul's dog wasn't eager for walks
Because his legs were thin as match stick stalks.

But all good things must come to an end
And these things happened when Paul went out and
Brought another canine friend, her name . . . Fi Fi.

Stacey-Leigh Skitt (11)
Windsor High School

My Poem

When I get out of bed I look out of my window and all of the
leaves have fallen off the trees and the ground is icy from the
cold. It makes me feel like my birthday is here but not for
another year. I say to myself as I put my new jumper on,
'Come and get your money off the table,'
Said a voice from downstairs.

Robert Lowe (11)
Windsor High School

ME AND MY SCHOOL

I go to Windsor
I get squashed
Any minute now, I'm gonna get lost.

There's the bell
I need to run
Down the stairs and here I come.

I go to Windsor
I get squashed
Any minute now, I'm gonna get lost.

Help me Miss
Where do I go?
My friends have left me, I'm really slow.

I go to Windsor
I get squashed
Any minute now, I'm gonna get lost!

Stacey Randle (11)
Windsor High School

HALLOWE'EN

H   is for Hallowe'en when I go trick or treating.
A   is for alligator that witches put in spells.
L   is for lights that sparkle in the night.
L   is for liquorice that I pile in my bag.
O   is for October that's when it's hallowe'en.
W   is for witches that spook you out.
E   is for evenings when I go out to hunt.
E   is for everyone that joins in the fun.
N   s for night where it all ends.

Kristina Ridley (11)
Windsor High School

CROSS-COUNTRY RUNNER

I'm at the starting post,
my heart is pumping fast,
my legs are weak with fear,
my stomach feels a little queer.

The race gun fires and
the fears disappear.
I need to do my best,
trainers thudding in the mud,
shouting voices in the crowd.

I'm not sure if my
legs will last.
I feel like turning back
I best go on and finish the
race even if I'm last!

Natalie Whyte (11)
Windsor High School

MILLENNIUM BUG

The Millennium Bug is here to stay
So it's time to sit and pray,
All it is, is a simple chip,
But it causes a lot of damage.
It lives on files from your computer system
Once you have got it you would wish you missed 'em.
So when you switch on your computer
Try and get rid of this terrible chip
Eating your files.
It's your last chance.

Sam Busher (11)
Windsor High School

I HAVE A DREAM

I have a dream,
That no one will be killed for who they are,
That there will be no wars.

I have a dream,
That all the people in the world will be friends,
Regardless of their colour or beliefs.

I have a dream,
That no one will ever starve from hunger,
Through other people's greed.

I have a dream,
That most of all peace will last
Throughout the next millennium.

Hannah Didlock (11)
Windsor High School

I HAD A DREAM

I had a dream
That I was big and famous
That I lived in a castle
With a dragon outside
Then a drawbridge went down with a clatter
Then it turned out it was a cat in the bin
I was asleep
I'd been dreaming
It couldn't be true because
I was in the dump.

Kara Sunburk (11)
Windsor High School

THE TEST

Everyone is holding on to their lives,
On the desk the test papers are delivered,
The whole class give nervous shivers.

I feel like a little ant preparing to
Climb on an elephant,
Finally, we are told to begin,
Number 1 was very easy,
2, 3 and 4 not too sure,
5 and 6 the answer I can fix,
I'm nearly there, just 4 to go,
What is it? What is it?
Oh I know.

Everyone gives out gleeful cheers,
Because they have come over their fears,
Hip, hip, hooray! Hip, hip, hooray!

Matthew Knowles (11)
Windsor High School

SCHOOL HALLOWE'EN DRESS

I made my way to Windsor
Dressed up like a vampire,
I went up to the teacher and said
'I don't know what to do?
Do you think it is a scare?'
The teacher said 'It's fine'
I walked in the class
And what a great big laugh.

Hollie Downes (11)
Windsor High School

I HAD A LOVELY RED BALLOON

I had a lovely red balloon.
I took it out to play.
The wind came rushing down the road
And carried it away.
Up, up it went higher than the sky
And Mrs Rook said 'Cor I've never seen
A red balloon above my nest before.'
Up, up it went past a smoking chimney
Stack. When the smoke had died
My red balloon was black.
As it sailed away I thought how funny
It would be if it should sail right
Round the world and then come back to me.

Kellie Kirton (12)
Windsor High School

LOVE

Love is a wonderful thing.
It makes me feel so alive.
You cannot stop thinking about
the one that you love.
Your heart starts to pound.
Sometimes I think of the
one that I love, the boy with
golden hair.
I cannot hide my love
anymore for he is the one I need.

Katie Bridgwater (12)
Windsor High School

MYSTERY POEM

One morning in May
We lined up to school,
In the usual way.
Well no, we didn't really,
Because the school wasn't there,
We lined up to where
The school had been.
There was nothing
It had all gone
And there wasn't a clue.
No hole, no scar,
You'd thought there might be.
A lot of cheering from the kids,
But there wasn't
They all just stood around
Wondering.
Not even talking much.
I wonder where the school did go,
Maybe it was stolen,
By a UFO.

Daniel James (11)
Windsor High School

SPACE IS

Space is big, bigger than anything.
Space is very dark, darker than you have seen.
Space is very mysterious, we don't know everything.
Space is unexplored we can't go everywhere.
Space is interesting you will like it.
Space goes on forever (it doesn't end).
Space is . . .

Adam Williams (11)
Windsor High School

LESSONS

Come on you horrible lot,
Get your books out
Draw this chart!
'Please sir, I've left my ruler at home.'
'You'll have to borrow Jo Jo's then
Hurry up Simon.'

'Come on you horrible lot
Get your books out
Write these words.'
'Miss, I've left my pencil at home!'
'Well write in pen then.'
'Oh please hurry up Jenny!'

'Come on you horrible, lot
Get the paints out
Draw a face.'
'Miss Jane threw paint at me!'
'Well go to the toilet and clean it up.
Come on, chop, chop!'

'Come on you horrible lot
Get out of my sight
The bell has gone
It's home for you
Don't forget your bag
Don't forget your homework
Oh please! Please go home.'

Elizabeth Payne (12)
Windsor High School

THE GHOST IN MY GARDEN

The ghost in my garden
Tickles my cheeks
He whispers so softly
As he quietly speaks.

The ghost in my garden,
He is free,
Nobody can see him
Except for me.

The ghost in my garden
Eats his tea
Down in the bushes
With me.

The ghost in my garden
He listens to me
Honest and truthful
That's what friends should be.

The ghost in my garden
Goes to bed
With the lawnmower and spade
Alone in the shed.

Jessica Parsons (11)
Windsor High School

DINNER TIME

The bell goes for dinner time
Rushing for the dinner line
The lovely smell of luscious chips
And there are also lovely dips.

When I go out to play with friends,
We play tig, the fun never ends.
When it comes to the end of dinner time
We go to the classroom, we're in a line.

Chris Willetts (11)
Windsor High School

BUGS

I like spiders or beetles
Or even caterpillars.
They're all different bugs
You can see,
Big or little ones.
You can find
Blue, green or yellow ones
Or even
Black, red and pink ones.
They are all different from one another.
They are all colours and sizes
Worms dig,
Spiders pin webs,
Ladybugs fly.
Caterpillars turn into butterflies and
Fly away,
Wasps sting you
Flies are annoying.
Bees collect flies,
Beetles are there,
But they are all still bugs.

Jamie Jackson (11)
Windsor High School

THREE-COURSE MEAL

T hree-course meals have anything.
H am, mushroom, sausage and beef
R adish, tomato, a lettuce leaf.
E at, eat, eat, galore,
E at, eat and eat some more.

C heese, mince, bolognese,
O ranges, bananas you don't know their age.
U gli fruit, apples, pears, egg and chicken,
R oasts, banana 'n' plums for picking.
S moked bacon, prawn cocktail
E normous potatoes dark and pale.

M ango, mayonnaise or tuna instead,
E at some cornflakes sat in bed.
A pple strudel custard on the side,
L ovely milk down throats it glides.

Andrew Crumpton (11)
Windsor High School

GIRLS VERSUS BOYS

Girls can do anything,
Boys can do nothing,
Just sit in the corner
And suck their thumbs.
Girls play football against the boys
The girls win because the boys are just toys.
Boys are boys and that is that
You can't change that, it's a fact.
Girls just rule,
Boys just drool
And that is the end of that.

Rebecca Owen (11)
Windsor High School

I'M A GIRL AND HE'S A BOY

I'm a girl
It's great so there
I've got brown eyes
And long brown hair.

I'm a girl
It's great so there
I get my sweets out
And start to share.

He's a boy
And he doesn't care
He's got blue eyes
And short blonde hair.

He's a boy
And he doesn't care
He gets his sweets out
And does not share.

Zana Vukasovic (11)
Windsor High School

ANIMALS

A nimals everywhere, some high in the trees,
N aughty squirrels burying nuts in the children's playground,
I n the park there is a stream where the fish like to swim,
M eanwhile the children play and owners walk their dogs,
A nd beside the stream, the children throw bricks in the water,
L ovely green grass, lovely green trees, this is how I
    would like the world to be.
S o everybody look after this beautiful world we're living in!

Samantha Coombes (11)
Windsor High School

ME AND WINDSOR HIGH SCHOOL

I am a girl,
So listen to me,
I am a girl
And I'm 4 ft 3.

I'm not very tall,
I'm quite, quite small,
My friend is called Ali
And she's very, very pally.

My tutor group is 7SGR
I hate it when the older ones say 'Aaahhh'
They say we are small,
They're very, very tall,
That's what I feel about Windsor High School.

Sophie West (11)
Windsor High School

THE SCHOOL TOILETS

They're horrible and really stink,
There's always toilet roll down the sink.
Graffiti covers the walls
It's amazing to see how many people love Paul!
It's not the highlight of your day when
You have to go during play
And maybe some day they'll tidy them up.
But until then that's our school toilets!

Holly Van Russelt (11)
Windsor High School

SUBJECTS AND TEACHERS

Behind those thick rimmed glasses
Lies a devil asleep!
What would you like to do now class?
How about . . . English . . . French or Science.
Let's do English
Maybe . . .
Let's do Science.
No!
What about French!
Okay.

Bonjour la classe,
Bonjour Madame!
Comment t'appelles tu?
Je m'appelle Richard.
Now it's time for . . . English!

Mrs Matchett and Mr Hackett are the best
But I'm not mentioning the rest!

Richard Parkes (12)
Windsor High School

THE TEACHER'S PET

The teachers pet is Claire Payne,
We used to think she walked funny until someone
                                        told us she was lame,
She brings an apple in a day to keep the teacher happy,
We all laugh that much, we sometimes need a nappy,
At least, at last she made a friend whose name was Anne Bell.
Everything Claire did wrong, she used to twit and tell,
This Claire Payne has not had much luck at all,
I'm going to make her my friend, let's have a game of basketball.

Mia McKay (11)
Windsor High School

JUST TOO MANY DAYS

Today I sat
My head down
As the teacher carries on her
Usual gobble.

Maths, Maths, Maths,
Just too many numbers.

The teacher writes all kinds of things,
As I daydream up at the wall,
'Jonathan' she calls out,
Phew it's only the register call.

English, English, English
Just too many verbs and nouns.

Well that's my weekly dose of school.

Jonathan Darby (11)
Windsor High School

TROUBLE

In trouble again,
Oh why?
Another detention,
Oh why?
Talking in class again,
Oh my!
Can't keep my mouth shut,
I do try,
Tomorrow I'll be good again,
Well I'll try!

Hannah Dempsey (11)
Windsor High School

SCHOOL POEM

The night was creeping on the ground
My teacher crept on the creaking floor and
Did not make a sound.
Until my teacher reached the classroom
Then one of my friends said
'Shall we change dooms?'
He threw some detentions and said
'Get back into the detention room,
Or I will give you a job
And guess what it is doing, the laundry,
Ha, ha, ha, ha, ha.
Now see who is laughing?
Ha, ha, ha, ha, ha.'

Emma Thorp (11)
Windsor High School

HIGH SCHOOL

The best bit of the day
Is having to go out to play.
The worst thing about the day,
Is to go home to do your homework
Each and every way.
There's too much to do.
The library you can go.
When you get to year eleven,
There's a big task to do! GCSE tests,
But you're not always the best.
It's college next.
There's a test every year,
It's almost getting near.

Timothy Deeley (11)
Windsor High School

THE TEACHERS

Behind the windows in the classroom,
There lay a disgraceful teacher,
The heart breaking words came out
Of the mouth,
'Let's get to work!'
I knew I shouldn't have come to school.

Teachers good, teachers bad,
This one's worst,
They give you detention,
Don't give merits
And really get up my nose.

Matchett, Hackett and Neville are the best,
I don't want to say who is worst!

Robert Hadley (11)
Windsor High School

THE CORRIDORS

Clashing and smashing in the corridors,
I can't see my own hands, let alone the dinner doors.
There's big year elevens trampling over people
And teachers ploughing through us all.
I can see a quick glimpse of the food,
Oh no! It's gone again, all I can see is
People jumping over each other.
It's just like a stampede of elephants,
I've never seen such a thing like this -
It's chaos!
Oh please let me out,
Oh please.

Jack Hudson (11)
Windsor High School

The School Fish

The school fish just lies in a dish full of water,
We give it food that it never eats
It doesn't like the fishy treats,
It really isn't very nice
We'd rather have some baby mice
I'd really like a great white shark
Or even a dog with a very loud bark
Some people say it's dead,
Other people say it's in bed.

Really I just think it's boring
I'd rather do some landscape drawing
Why didn't we get a cat
Or a snake or a mole or a little smelly rat
I'd love to have a hamster, eating from its dish,
But no, everyone ignored me,
We had to get a fish.

Edward Geater (11)
Windsor High School

Body Boarding

You clamber over the rocks to get to the sea line,
You start to walk into the sea,
The fearsome waves crash down on the sea,
You start swimming after the wave, the adrenaline rush starts
You caught the wave
You start to rush
Then you do it all over again.

Philip Harrold (11)
Windsor High School

AMOS! MY SLOBERCHOPPY DOGGY

How I love my dog so sweet,
It licks my ears, it licks my feet.
Always so playful, always so kind,
I feed it on chicken and pigs behind.
I like the way it lies on my bed,
It drools on my quilt, while I stroke its head.
How it protects me when I take it on walks.
Growls at the people, the ones that stalk.
When he's naughty, I give him a smack
When he's good I scratch his back.
There are some bad points though, I must say
You have to take it on walks every day.
When it's a pup you might like it less
'Cause every day you have to clean up its mess!
So if you want a dog, think carefully please,
'Cause what will you do when it gets fleas?
But my dog called Amos is my best friend
From the day that I've had him, the fun does not end.

Jake Croft (11)
Windsor High School

I WILL ACHIEVE

I'm gonna be a fashion designer.
With zer goatee beards and blue shaded glasses.

I will achieve.

Zey are so fashionable with zer expensive pinstripes.
Zey have lots and lots and loads of money.

I will achieve.

Me and ma friends will go valking,
Valking down the rich roads of London signing
Signing autographs vor all around.

I will achieve.

Ya I vill say ven I'm earning millions, I knew I would.

I have achieved.

Harry Denning (11)
Windsor High School

MY EMBARRASSING LIFE AT WINDSOR

For girl's basketball,
For boy's football,
All mixed together they are so much fun,
Rugby, gymnastics,
Tie ups those elastics
You are gonna have lots of fun
Plumb tart, raspberry heart,
Puddings galore,
Don't bring no more,
Dinner today don't have to pay
Until tomorrow, glub, glub,
Homework, homework,
Please no more,
Or I'll fly away
School is really OK.

Heather Reeves (11)
Windsor High School

WHY MATHS?

Maths, maths, why maths?
I can't see any point in it.
Just a load of numbers
Adding and taking away.

Maths, maths, why maths?
Area and perimeter today
That's just lots of adding
And multiplying again.

Maths, maths, why maths?
Who on earth invented it?
Couldn't they have invented
Something that is much more fun.

Maths, maths, why maths?
How come it has to be nearly every day.
Can't we have a day off
After confusing our brains.

Maths, maths, why maths?
Isn't there anything more fun
Like English, PE or even Drama,
Art, anything but
Maths.

Rosie Mason (11)
Windsor High School

THE MURDER

It's Saturday night, it's getting dark,
I'm walking slowly in the park
And suddenly I hear a shout,
I turn quite sharp and look about,
My heart is beating really fast,
Could this breath be my last?
I'm running from tree to tree,
I don't know what I think I will see
And suddenly I hear a crack,
I stop dead in my track.
I take a step back and have a look,
It's probably evidence of who's the crook
And then I see something in the fog,
Something that looks a lot like a log.
I go a bit closer and then I see,
It's not a log, it's a human body.
I hear a rustle in the bush,
A person's running, they're in a rush.
I take a close look to see who it is,
In case you don't know I'm Inspector Bis.
The body is Mr Crow
And the murderer is a man, I know.
But the only two people who hate Mr Crow,
Are Mr Son and Mr Low.
Do you know how to solve this crime?
It's puzzling me, I'm losing my mind.

Victoria Heath (12)
Windsor High School

SCHOOL DINNERS

When the bell goes we all pour
Down the corridors we crawl.
Down the corridors we fall
Down to the dining hall, we all pour.

For school dinners that are great
But we hope we don't make a mistake.
Cardboard chips and some monster burgers
Cheesy pizza and beefy burgers.

These are the things we like most
Going for school dinners we like the best.
It makes me happy to be here
I wish all of you could be here!

Alex Laurent (11)
Windsor High School

FOOTBALL

Football is a lot of fun especially when you win,
But when you lose it's not so good.
When you draw it is OK.
You get one point for a draw,
But 3 points for a win.
It is good to score a goal
But then good to set one up
When you score an own goal it's still a goal.
But on the wrong side
And you will be in for a telling off.
If you get a yellow card it's not so bad,
But if you get a red card you're in for a scare!

James Picketts (11)
Windsor High School

GOING OUT

I went to a disco
All the tills were crashing.
People were bashing
The glasses were clashing
With all the bashing.
The music was loud
Everyone was proud
There were loads of crowds
Around the toilets.
The need of the night came
It was just like a hot flame
People were talking and
Walking and some more
Were even sulking.

Jade Hill (11)
Windsor High School

IN THE FUTURE

In the future we might make contact with aliens,
In the future we might live on Mars,
In the future we might communicate in holograms,
In the future cars might drive themselves,
In the future we might play virtual reality games in arcades,
In the future the world might be taken over by aliens,
In the future we might be injected with a food capsule and
We won't have to eat for the rest of our lives,
I hope not but in the future the world might explode,
Who knows what the future holds?

James Simpson (11)
Windsor High School

THE MILLENNIUM DOME

Look at the great white Millennium Dome
See how over the year it has grown.
From the rocky foundations we had seen,
To a great white entertainment machine,
As the murky water of the Thames flows by.
Ticket holders will have the time of their lives.
Everything's there, done just for you,
Blackadder's on and there's a huge body too!
As the people of London go on their way,
The workers prepare for the one big day.
The Dome has cost millions from the nations pocket
But who knows if it will all be worth it?
On the big day the Dome will be packed
And I can't think of anything to rhyme with that!
Everyone counts down in one accord
Though some are at home, thoroughly bored.
Midnight comes, everyone cheers
Although there are ones who cover their ears.
The time is here, the Millennium's come
And in the moonlight the Dome just shone.

Ross Cunningham (11)
Windsor High School

SCHOOL DINNERS

Class has finished
The bell has gone
It's dinner time for everyone.

There's hustle and bustle
In the corridor
Racing to get to the queue.

We grab our plates
And fill them up with
Chips and burgers.

And then we rush to find a place
With our mates.
Trays are stacked
And we walk out.
No need to rush.

Victoria Byng (11)
Windsor High School

AUTUMN

The wind blows against
my cheek and the leaves
on the floor are in a gathering.
All of them crunching as my
worn-in leather walking boots
trample all over them.

The low autumnal sun
reflects off a pain of
glass into my widely opened
eyes. My arms have goosebumps
on them and there are grazed
places on my small outstretched hand.

I gathered two sticks together
and threw them as far
as I could and one
after the other, they
flew into the distance.

James Sayer (11)
Windsor High School

MILLENNIUM

The millennium is coming in a couple of months
Everybody is very excited and anxious too,
I hope nobody gets the mumps
I am praying the sky will be blue.
So I can go and play with my mates.
There will be lots of parties and millennium fates
Everybody is worrying about the Millennium Bug
I am not, I think it is a lie,
I just sit there and shrug.
I can't wait until midnight strikes
All the party poppers go off
And then for the rest of the night
Well we will have to wait and see.

Maisie Denning (11)
Windsor High School

TEACHERS

Teachers, teachers everywhere
Up my nose and in my hair,
I see one every single day,
Morning, lunch and even play!

They guard the tuck shop,
The corridors too,
They even pop their heads
Around the door of the loo!

Wherever I go,
Whatever I see
There always seems to be one
Waiting for me!

Natalie Roberts (11)
Windsor High School

MILLENNIUM

The millennium's coming,
People are getting excited,
People are also worried about the
Millennium Bug.
But I'm not worried
I'm ready to party.

It will be a once in a lifetime
Experience, that nobody will
Ever experience twice.

There are people buying fireworks,
Food, party hats etc.

Every day people booking to stay in
The Millennium Dome.

It's all fun and it's getting closer every day!

It will soon be here and it will soon be gone.

New Years Eve people are
Preparing food for the parties,
The next day blowing balloons
Up and putting streamers and banners up
And now let's party the night away!

Jessica Hill (11)
Windsor High School